WITNESS:

The World
Since Hiroshima

Books by Roger Rosenblatt

→》》 《《←

BLACK FICTION

CHILDREN OF WAR

WITNESS: THE WORLD SINCE HIROSHIMA

WITNESS:

The World Since Hiroshima

ROGER ROSENBLATT

Little, Brown and Company · Boston · Toronto

LIBRARY OF CONGRESS CATALOG CARD NO. 85-45462

FIRST EDITION

→》》 《《←

*All of the material in this book
originally appeared in* Time *magazine.*

BP
DESIGNED BY JEANNE F. ABBOUD

*Published simultaneously in Canada
by Little, Brown & Company (Canada) Limited*

PRINTED IN THE UNITED STATES OF AMERICA

To
Ray Cave

⇥⇥ ⇤⇤

⇒⇒ CONTENTS ⇐⇐

WITNESS:
The World
Since Hiroshima

⇥⇥ INTRODUCTION ⇤⇤

Early on the morning of Aug. 6, 1945, the *Enola Gay,* named for the pilot's mother, cut east to west across the rivers of Hiroshima, opened its hatches, and an atom bomb fell free. From that moment to this, nothing has ever been the same in the world. The people of Hiroshima, the course of World War II, subsequent wars, subsequent peace, the position of science, the role of the military, international politics, the nature of knowledge, art, culture, the conduct of lives: all changed. Other ages in history were characterized by heroes or by ideas. The atomic age is characterized by a weapon and a threat.

Forty years later, what is Hiroshima? What happened there to make it impossible for the world to turn back? How has the Bomb served the world, and how is the world supposed to live with it?

Here are four views of what occurred on and after Aug. 6, 1945. Not four sides of an argument, but four perspectives on a reality. The first view is that of a survivor of the bombing who is now the director of the Hiroshima Peace Memorial Museum. What he saw was the suffering of people and the destruction of a city. The second view is that of a physicist who witnessed the first successful nuclear chain-reaction experiment in Chicago in 1942, worked on the Bomb at the Los Alamos laboratory and flew in the yield-measuring instrument plane beside the *Enola Gay*. Later he was the director of Los Alamos. What he saw was the effort of American scientists to win the war and the developing partnership of science and the military.

The third view is that of a U.S. President, one of eight Americans in history to have the power to wield nuclear weapons. What he saw after Hiroshima was a revolution in world politics and in the nature of the presidency. The fourth is a view of how the Bomb affected American thought and culture. What the people saw after Hiroshima was a fearful vision of the future.

Not only do these views sometimes clash with one another, there are doubts and contradictions within each of them. Yet individual views are all that is left of this singular event, since the rubble of Hiroshima has long been bulldozed away, the dead cremated, the air blown clean. Today on streets over which the Bomb's cloud rose like a red-purple flower are coffeehouses where Mozart is played, gilded hotels with blazing chandeliers, COKE IS IT signs and the headquarters of the Mazda corporation. Everything faces forward, except that the name of the city can never be mentioned without invoking a past to which everyone is attached, and an immediate private silence. Hiroshima survives in the mind, which broods, denies, forgets and eventually must deal with what it saw.

WHAT
THE BOY SAW

When Yoshitaka Kawamoto came to, the classroom was very dark, and he was lying under the debris of the crushed school building. In those days most Japanese buildings were made of wood; when the Bomb dropped, all but one or two of the structures that stood near the hypocenter of the explosion were flattened like paper hats. Kawamoto's school, the Hiroshima Prefectural First Middle School, stood only 800 meters, a mere half-mile, from the hypocenter. Two-thirds of his classmates were killed instantly where they sat at their desks. Some who survived were weeping and calling for their mothers. Others began singing the school song to bolster their courage and to let passersby know that the 13-year-olds were still alive.

"But then the singing and the cries grew weaker. My

classmates were dying one by one. That made me very frightened. I struggled to free myself from the broken fragments, and looked around. I thought that gas tanks had exploded. Through a hole in the roof I could see clouds swirling in a cone; some were black, some pink. There were fires in the middle of the clouds. I checked my body. Three upper teeth were chipped off; perhaps a roof tile had hit me. My left arm was pierced by a piece of wood that stuck in my flesh like an arrow. Unable to pull it out, I tied a tourniquet around my upper arm to stanch the flow of blood. I had no other injuries, but I did not run away. We were taught that it was cowardly to desert one's class-mates. So I crawled about the rubble, calling, 'Is there any-one alive?'

"Then I saw an arm shifting under planks of wood. Ota, my friend, was moving. But I could see that his back was broken, and I had to pull him up into the clear. Ota was looking at me with his left eye. His right eyeball was hanging from his face. I think he said something, but I could not make it out. Pieces of nails were stuck on his lips. He took a student handbook from his pocket. I asked, 'Do you want me to give this to your mother?' Ota nodded. A moment later he died. By now the school was engulfed in flames. I started to walk away, and then looked back. Ota was staring at me with his one good eye. I can still see that eye in the dark."

So began Kawamoto's morning, Aug. 6, 1945. Yoshi-taka Kawamoto is 53 today, a small, solid man who dresses formally in blue or brown suits and carries himself with a quick-moving dignity. When he tells the story of what happened 40 years ago, however, he can become a 13-year-old on the spot—suddenly springing from a chair to strike a military pose, demonstrating a march step, or hunching down like a shortstop. In his office he sang the school song that was sung by his classmates the morning of the bombing. As he did, he rose automatically and snapped to attention, chin tucked, eyes forward:

The rain pours white against the Hiroshima evening.
Colors fade on petals just past full bloom,
Spring is passing.
But we stand firm, our dreams of prosperity unfading.

Only in the past two years, since he was appointed director of the Hiroshima Peace Memorial Museum, has Kawamoto begun to tell the story of his days of survival. Before then he did not want publicly to declare himself a *hibakusha,* a survivor of the bombing. He is aware of the unspoken stigma attached to being a *hibakusha,* that people often treat the survivors with a sort of sympathetic shunning. It is also unlike Kawamoto to do anything without a clearly defined reason. The museum directorship provided a reason. Kawamoto now recounts his experiences to museum visitors and groups of schoolchildren. He believes in his new role; people must know the facts, he says. At the same time, this retelling of the August days has caused Kawamoto deep uneasiness. He had given little thought to Ota before the past two years. Now Ota appears in his dreams. Kawamoto explains that much guilt is connected to surviving the bombing. In the days following Aug. 6, he lost Ota's student handbook.

Kawamoto spoke of that time, Aug. 6-11, during a recent five-day period, telling part of his story in his office across the hall from the Peace Museum, and the rest "on location," in various places where the story occurred. His office and the museum are in a long, silvery modern building that looks like a harmonica, situated at the broad end of the triangular Peace Memorial Park. At the point of the triangle sits the Aioi Bridge, a T-shaped structure span ning the Honkawa, the river that served as the aiming point for the *Enola Gay*. (The Bomb missed by only a block or two.) Between the point and the broad end of the trian- gular park lies a grassy area dotted with various memorials to peace or to specific victims of the bombing, the most sought-out of which is a rocket-shaped sculpture dedicat- ed to a little girl who in 1955 died of leukemia attributed to radiation poisoning. According to one account, the girl made more than 900 paper cranes before she died, trust- ing that if she completed 1,000, her life would be spared. In Japan there is an old belief that a crane can live for 1,000 years, and that if you fold 1,000 paper cranes, they will protect you from illness. Thousands of green, red and yel- low paper cranes made by schoolchildren billow out from under the rocket like the undergarments of a skirt.

At the center of the Peace Park is a stone cenotaph that looks like a covered wagon from the American prairie. It contains the names of the Hiroshima dead who have been identified—113,000 names to date. In an oblong pool be- fore the cenotaph burns an "eternal flame" in an odd me- tallic structure resembling a headless figure with its arms extended; the flame burns where the head would be. On either side of the pool are red-orange and pink roses of enormous size, and trees that look as if they were formed by stacking bulbous tire-shaped hedges on top of one another. On a typical afternoon couples stroll, mothers push babies, children hand out peace buttons, pigeons swoop in low arcs like confetti, then up again over the water, the monuments, the museum.

The area's most recognizable structure is what is now called the Atomic Bomb Dome, originally Hiroshima Prefecture's Industrial Promotion Hall, a sort of chamber of commerce building and exhibition hall in 1945. The remains stand just outside the point of the park, across the Aioi Bridge. This shell is Hiroshima's Eiffel Tower, its Statue of Liberty. Where the dome rose, only the supporting beams remain, a giant hairnet capping four floors of vacant gray walls, much of their outer skin peeled away, exposing patches of brick. The interior floors are also gone, making the entire structure an accidental atrium. A front doorway leads to nowhere. A metal spiral staircase ascends to nothing. A pillar lies on its side, wires springing like wild hairs.

Yet not the dome nor the Peace Park nor the monuments—and there are dozens of monuments to victims throughout the city—give any real feeling of the devastation of Aug. 6, 1945. Even the film that is shown visitors to the Peace Museum displays less sadness and horror than one would expect, in spite of the pictures of scorched children and hairless women lying listless in hospital beds. Far more affecting is a three- to five-minute 16-mm movie in Kawamoto's possession that shows Hiroshima in 1936: men who still dressed in kimono; elegant women scooting rapidly through the streets of a shopping district; cherry blossoms; a fleeting glimpse of the Atomic Bomb Dome as it looked originally: fat, Victorian and official.

It is the ordinariness of the city that creates the sense of loss; what a normally pleasant city Hiroshima was before the bombing, what a normally pleasant city it is today. On any summer morning, the Hiroshima Carp take infield practice in the baseball stadium; fashionably dressed young men and women walk purposefully to work; traffic builds on the city's bridges. If you would picture the layout of the center of Hiroshima, which covers much of the ground of Kawamoto's story, place your right hand palm down on a flat surface with your fingers spread wide. Your fingers are rivers. On the land between your third and fourth fingers lies the Peace Park. Between your fourth and fifth fingers Kawamoto's school was situated. The heel of your hand is Hiroshima Bay, and beyond your fingertips lie mountains and countryside.

Between your second and third fingers is where the *Enola Gay* dropped the Bomb at 8:15 a.m. on Aug. 6. Once relieved of its nearly 9,000-lb. burden, the plane thrust upward, jerking the heads of the crew. The B-29 made a 60° dive and a 158° right turn. Forty-three seconds after the Bomb was released, it detonated. The crew members watched it explode in a red core below them. Then they headed back to base, the tiny island of Tinian in the Northern Marianas, 1,600 miles to the south.

That morning had begun routinely for Kawamoto. At the time, he was living with his mother and his younger brother in Ono, now a growing suburb of 30,000, then a fishing village of fewer than 10,000, about 30 kilometers outside Hiroshima, across Hiroshima Bay. Mrs. Kawamoto had taken her two boys to Ono one year before, after her husband, an engineer, had been killed in a freak accident in an electrical factory. Until then the Kawamotos had been living in the nearby village of Kuba, where Yoshitaka and his friends swam out long distances in the bay. "They called us 'children of the sea.' " Sailors from German U-boats would wave to the boys from the subs. Kuba was a wonderful town to grow up in, Kawamoto says, a place of frogs and dragonflies. Boys would test their courage in the graveyard at night. "In the daytime we wore uniforms, but at night we put on kimono. In the graveyard the hem of your kimono could get caught on a bush. It would feel like a hand tugging you down."

In Ono the morning routine was this: at 6, Kawamoto would rise, put on his school uniform, and walk down the hill to catch the train for Hiroshima. Monday, Aug. 6, was very hot, even that early in the day, and Kawamoto was tired. All the children his age had been conscripted by the military to clear firebreaks in Hiroshima, areas of escape or safety in case fires spread after bombing raids. Not that there had ever been major bombing raids on Hiroshima. While Tokyo and Osaka were being fire bombed by the Americans in March, Hiroshima was relatively untouched, save for two bombing incidents in March and April, the second of which tore a huge hole in a street near Kawamoto's school.

Aug. 6 had in fact begun with an air-raid alert for the city just after 7, but the B-29 soon passed over, and the all

16   WITNESS:

clear was sounded. This was the weather plane that advised the *Enola Gay* that the target was open. Schoolchildren looked forward to air-raid alerts, which allowed them to stop working. Kawamoto said goodbye to his mother, who told him to take care of himself. He plonked a shovel on his shoulder and strode soldier-like toward the railway station.

When the train arrived at the West Hiroshima station, Kawamoto and the other first-year boys gathered outside and, commanded by the senior boys, jogged in formation about two kilometers to the school. They jogged across the Shin Koi Bridge over the Ota River spillway, across a slim space of land to another bridge, which spanned the Tenma River, across another strip of land and the Nishi Heiwa Bridge over the Honkawa, finally crossing the Heiwa Bridge over the Motoyasu River. About 100 meters from the school gate, Kawamoto and his classmates were ordered to halt and march regimentally the rest of the way.

"We arrived at school at 7:45 a.m. Morning assembly would begin in the schoolyard promptly at 8. As was our custom, we began the day by bowing to the picture of the Emperor, and then proceeded to our classroom, where we recited the instructions for soldiers. These were rules of conduct, lessons that soldiers were always to obey. Fifteen minutes was never enough time to recite those lessons, but we could not be late for the 8 a.m. assembly. We went out into the yard and stood in rows. I saw B-29s flying overhead, and I thought, 'Maybe we won't have to work.' The head teacher spoke and gave us instructions for the day. Leaving assembly, we were divided into two groups: odd-

and even-numbered classes. The odd-numbered classes
were to take the first shift clearing firebreaks. The even-
numbered classes went inside to begin regular school-
work. I was in the even-numbered group.

"In the classroom we immediately went to our desks.
The desks were attached to chairs; we told ourselves that
they were the same kind of desks used in the United States
I had a special feeling for my desk. There was a space between the desk and the chair that we could dive under in an
air raid. We also had 'bulletproof' helmets, which were not
bulletproof and not really helmets, but rather pointed hats
of thick cloth made by our mothers. The senior boys ordered us to close our eyes and meditate. I closed my eyes,
but did not meditate; I was only wondering if the seniors
were going to hit us. They were always clouting us for one
thing or another. I practiced making the kind of face that
did not look as if it ought to be hit." Kawamoto demon-
strates the expression of a blank mask.

"Then the seniors went out of the classroom, leaving
the younger boys to meditate on their own. I opened my
eyes. A boy named Fujimoto—I think his father was a doctor—was seated by the window. He called out, 'Look! A
B-29!' My classmates kept meditating, but I was very curious, so I started to go toward the window. That was when
the flash hit. I heard no sound. It was a flash like lightning.
The air was shimmering, the way a television screen shim-
mers when it is out of order."

Then unconsciousness. Then the school song. Then
Ota.

"Remember, I had only been in the middle school four

months, like all first-year boys; not enough time to make many friends. Ota and I became friends because we were both short, and since students were allotted seats according to their height, Ota and I were placed beside each other in the first row. I admired Ota very much. I was just a country boy, but Ota was polished and handsome, the kind of fellow I had always thought of as the perfect city boy. White skin, clearly defined eyebrows, a Western-type nose, not a flattish one like mine. The whites of his eyes always sparkled. And he had a husky, manly voice. Everyone looked up to him because he was so articulate. He was fun too, a very special boy.

"I left him in the fire and went out into the playground. The playground was covered with a thick, dark layer of smoke. I could see the blue sky filter through from place to place. I did not know which way to run. Out of the flames and noise, I heard a voice cry, 'Run into the wind. Run into the wind.' I picked up a fistful of sand—to this day I do not know how I thought to do this—and tossed the sand in the air to see which way the wind was blowing. There was fire everywhere. Bodies lay dead or writhing all over the playground.

"Then I saw the head teacher. So severe were his burns, I could not recognize his face, only his voice. He wore nothing but a pair of undershorts, and he was dragging a cart with some of my classmates lying on it. I helped drag the cart, but the going was extremely slow and difficult. We had to lift the cart over the other bodies, and those who were still alive grabbed at our ankles and begged for help. We had to push bodies aside to clear a path. Finally, we reached a point safe from the fires. We found several tin cans of oil. I dipped a towel in the oil and dabbed my classmates' wounds. The road was heating up terribly, either because of the sunlight or because of the bomb. [The bomb emitted a land temperature in that area of at least 3000° C, or 5400° F, twice the heat required to melt iron.] The head teacher and I did not talk. I was too tired to talk. I only wanted water. Two students in the cart died before my eyes."

Kawamoto has been telling this part of his story standing in a school playground that was built where his old school playground used to be. It is only four or five blocks from his office. The new playground is much larger than the old one, Kawamoto says. There are tennis courts on one side; a soccer game is in progress; over in a corner a girl puts a shot while a friend measures the distances. Kawamoto observes that children today are less disciplined than in his generation. He speaks fondly of the strong sense of unity among his classmates, how they stuck together against both the seniors and the military officers assigned to the school to conduct military exercises.

"The officers also oversaw our lunches. Our lunches usually consisted of 'Japanese flags'—a bowl of rice with a red plum in the center, the design of the national flag. But if we had too much white rice, we were hit; white rice was a sign of luxury. If we had a mixture of rice and wheat, with more wheat than rice, that was O.K. Country boys had more white rice, of course, so we were hit quite often—either for that or for finishing our lunches too quickly. We were supposed to take a full hour with our rice, so we

would gobble it up at first, and then slow down, trying to
stretch out the hour. One of our military officers was especially strict, a real tyrant. He was in school the day of the
bombing. I saw him months later working in the black mar
ket, pounding a counter in the street to attract customers. '

Kawamoto did not like having the military around his
school, but he appreciates the military values of discipline.
He connects discipline with self-knowledge. Once, when
he was a very small boy, his father took him in a boat out
into the bay and threw him in, to teach the boy to swim.
Kawamoto struggled and tried to grab the side of the boat,
but his father pushed him off with a pole. Only when the
boy sank did his father pull him back. "I asked him why he
did not help me sooner. I thought my father was trying to
drown me. Later I understood that he was really trying to
save me, that I would only learn to swim if I came that close
to death."

Of the modern generation Kawamoto says it does not
possess "the kind of heart that knows how to stare into itself and discover its own strength. *Onore o shiru:* to know
oneself. It is essential. People today live too much by their
individual desires, and so are bound to repeat the mistakes
of the past. One must vow not to repeat those mistakes.
Unless you know yourself, you cannot make a vow that
counts."

In the Peace Museum now, Kawamoto uses a long
wooden pointer to indicate, in a large circular panorama,
the route of the rest of his escape. Above the center of the
panorama a bright red ball representing the hypocenter
hangs by a cord. Kawamoto touches the pointer to the area

of the playground, then moves it out into the city, away
from the hypocenter, toward the Kyobashi River and the
Miyuki Bridge.

"We were trying to get away from the fires and head for
the river. On the way, I lost sight of my teacher and proceeded alone. People burned too severely to survive
grabbed at me as I went along. Those who could walk
stumbled over the bodies; they wore tatters and were covered with ash. I saw a living baby clinging to the breasts of
its dead mother. I saw another child of three or four beating her dead mother with her fists. Perhaps she did not
know that her mother was dead and in desperation and
confusion was trying to wake her up.

"Near the Miyuki Bridge I met my classmate Kimura.
Kimura belonged to the odd-numbered group, so he had
been working in the streets when the bomb went off. His
face was charred. He lived in West Hiroshima, and he said
he was going home, which meant that he was heading back
toward the direction of the hypocenter. I told him that it
was impossible to go back, that the area was all in flames.
He was delirious and would not listen to me. He only re-
peated, 'I want to go home. I want to go home.' He walked
away toward the flames. Later his family could not locate
his ashes."

During the war people kept their own reservoirs in case
of fires. The water in these reservoirs lay filthy and stag-
nant through the year, but Kawamoto was desperately
thirsty. He started toward one of the reservoirs, but saw
that people were lying dead, half in, half out of the water.
Coming to the Miyuki Bridge at last, he leaped down the

steep stone steps, stumbling over others plummeting down. There was a logjam of bodies at the base of the steps. "I was so scared." He tried to drink the muddy water, but spit it out. He clambered up the riverbank.

"I lay on my back in the heat. There was no shade to cool me. Thick clouds were billowing above my head. It was a thunderhead. Fires glowed in the clouds. The sky was dark. I thought, 'I will never see my mother again.' Then I passed out."

Much of what Kawamoto saw between the school playground and the Miyuki Bridge is exhibited in the museum he directs. It is after hours now, so he is free to move easily from display case to display case, using one exhibit or another to illustrate his story. During regular hours the museum is packed with schoolchildren in uniform, pressing their noses against the windows of the cases; chattering; some horseplay from the bigger boys. On display is all that became of Hiroshima once the bomb dropped, along with historical memorabilia such as the directive from Lieut. General Carl Spaatz, commander in chief of the U.S. Strategic Air Force, ordering that the city be bombed; a large photo of the A-bomb known as "Little Boy," looking like a sea mammal in profile; messages of resolve or condolence from distinguished visitors; leaflets dropped by the Americans in early August 1945 that warned of some general disaster but not of the A-bomb specifically. "The Americans did warn Nagasaki about the Bomb, but not Hiroshima," says Kawamoto. "It made no difference anyway. Our military ordered the people not to read any of the leaflets, so none of our citizens knew what was coming."

Strange objects fill the display cases: testaments to the Bomb's effects on ordinary things. A twisted beam from a seven-story building; a charred tobacco pipe; a melted lump of coins; a mass of nails, of sake cups. A watch stopped at exactly 8:16 was found in the sands of the Motoyasu River. A horse is on display; its legs are missing. One case contains hair that had fallen in a clump on the ground. (Kawamoto's hair fell out after six weeks, but two months later it grew back again.) Another case contains black fingernails two or three inches in length that had grown on a hand where the skin was entirely burned off. The black nails had blood vessels in them; nothing like them was ever seen before.

And photographs of the suffering, their burned backs looking like topographical maps. And shadows of vaporized people that remained on streets after the people disappeared. And a wall streaked with "black rain," the large radioactive raindrops that fell shortly after the explosion.

The displays that touch Kawamoto most deeply are those of a middle-school uniform, much like his own, the jacket torn with one sleeve missing; and of wax models of victims walking as if stunned or asleep, their arms held out in front of them. Their skin hangs loose on their bones like ill-fitting clothing. Their real clothes are rags. In the display case they stand blank-eyed against a backdrop of a wasteland of ashes and a fire-streaked sky. "It is the way people really looked," Kawamoto says. "They did not seem to walk voluntarily; they appeared to be pushed.

"When I regained consciousness, I found myself lying in a warehouse, which was turned into a hospital, near the

Ujina port. The Ujina port is at a good distance from the
Miyuki Bridge. Soldiers had carried me to the warehouse.
There I waited. I remembered my fear at the sight of the
bodies in the river. I saw not a single fish. That river was
always full of fish. The whole area between my school and
the Miyuki Bridge had looked so different. That was where
Hiroshima University had stood. A railroad operated in
that neighborhood. A Red Cross hospital had been there
too. All gone. Children lay in the arms of dead parents,
parents carried the bodies of dead children. The soldiers
who brought me to the warehouse told of seeing a horse
killed on the spot where it stood during the flash. There
were no marks or wounds on the animal. It had died in its
tracks of shock or of a scorching wind.

"It was about 7 in the evening when I came to. It had
taken me 2½ hours to get from the playground to the
Miyuki Bridge, and this was eight or nine hours later, so I
had lain unconscious for a very long time. The warehouse
at Ujina ordinarily was used to store food for the soldiers.
Now it stored people, who sat dazed with their backs to the
walls. The first thing I saw on coming to was a soldier's
face looking into mine. He gave me an affectionate pat on
the head. Perhaps it was he who removed the piece of
wood from my arm, for the wood was gone now, and my
arm was in great pain. Another soldier who had medical
training was working his way around the warehouse, going
from victim to victim. When he came over to me I asked for
water, but he refused. They were only giving water to the
dying. By that I knew that I was expected to recover. The
first soldier came by and placed a piece of ice in my mouth.

I shall never forget his kindness.

"It was he who told me how I had happened to come to the warehouse. The people who originally found me by the river-bank thought I was dead, so they tossed me on top of a stack of bodies that they were about to set afire for cremation. Somehow my body slid off the pile. When a soldier tried to heave me back on top, he grabbed me by the wrist and felt my pulse."

Throughout the day, Mrs. Kawamoto had been frantic for news of her son. She had made an attempt to get into Hiroshima by train, but was turned back at the West Hiroshima station. The morning of Aug. 7 she made a second attempt, but this time the railway station was roped off. The next day she went to the schools in the towns around Ono; she heard that bomb victims had been brought to these schools, which, like the warehouse in Ujina, had been turned into hospitals. On Aug. 9 she got word that her son was alive on one of the islands outside the city, but she did not know where. With a group of neighbors who were also searching for their children, she hired a fishing boat to search the islands around Hiroshima.

"The soldiers tried to place me on a boat headed for the island of Ninoshima, but the people on the boat rejected me; they were already overloaded with passengers. The soldiers put me on another boat headed for the peninsula of Taibi. On Taibi I was placed in a tent that was otherwise occupied only by women. I suppose they did this because I was a child. Some of the women were with babies. Some of the women were half naked. Some showed no external wounds, but they had gone crazy from the bombing or from being parted from their families. They clung to the legs of the soldiers, imploring them, 'Where are my children?' The younger women, distraught, began climbing the tent poles, crying, 'Mother! Mother!' I could not sleep that night, or the next day, or even the next. The women cried for two days, but on the third, they were too exhaust ed to cry.

"The second day on Taibi, we had an air-raid alert, a false alarm. Those who could, walked to a shelter. Most people were too weak to stand. They urinated and defecated where they were lying. Soldiers, their eyes red with fatigue, passed around canned oranges. But I could not eat; I could not bear the smell in the tent. My face was burning with fever, and my eyes and lips grew swollen. By now my arm was in terrible pain, and finally a soldier took me to a doctor. The doctor wanted to amputate, but the soldier said, 'This boy is only 13. He has lots of things to do for our country. Please don't cut off his arm.' "

To which the doctor agreed, but said that he could not guarantee Kawamoto's life. Then he disinfected the wound. "I was not afraid now. I was sure I was going to live."

Kawamoto got word to his mother from Taibi. He did so indirectly, by invoking the name of a relative, a principal of a military school who was a powerful man in the military. A soldier, impressed by the name, called the village hall in Ono, saying that Kawamoto was alive, though he did not mention Taibi. That was when Mrs. Kawamoto hired the boat and began her search of the islands. Meanwhile, Kawamoto returned to the tent and waited, not knowing whether his mother had received his message or not. He began to get some sleep on Aug. 9, sleeping heavily for several hours at a time in the dark tent, lit only by candles, half waking when the women screamed.

In the Buddhist graveyard at Kuba, Kawamoto walks among the block-shaped tombstones and looks down from the steep hill at Hiroshima Bay, where he swam as a child. This was the graveyard where he and the other boys used to test their courage: "In the daytime we would come up here and leave some personal belonging. In the night we would retrieve it, which would prove to the others that we were here."

"There were mysterious stories about all these hills," he says, stories of tanuki, strange raccoon-dogs invested with mischievous, magical powers. He tells of a boy who used to go up into the mountains for birds' eggs; the birds nested in the mountains' muddy surface. "One day he asked me to go with him, but I was busy. By evening he had not returned home. His parents were very concerned, and they organized a search party. When the search party came upon the boy, they found him walking in a huge circle, round and round. He kept repeating, 'I have grown taller. My legs are long.' Everyone assumed that a tanuki had put a spell on him.

"Foxes were also supposed to be magical and troublesome. My grandfather used to tell me of a day he was walking along the 'beast path' of a mountain, a path between villages that foxes were thought to frequent. My grandfather was carrying a *bentō,* a box lunch; foxes were known to love *bentō.* Walking along, he suddenly heard the sound of straw shoes trudging in the sand behind him—*sarrah, sarrah, sarrah*. My grandfather looked back and saw what appeared to be a peasant girl in a dress, a shawl and sandals. But foxes were known to wear such disguises. One way to be sure was to see how the creature crossed water. If it stepped across, it was a peasant girl; if it jumped, it was a fox. When my grandfather came to a stream, he crossed quickly, hid and watched his pursuer. Sure enough the 'peasant girl' jumped the stream. I loved to hear that kind of story from my grandparents."

Reading the names on the Buddhist tombstones, Kawamoto points out those of the families he knew. He keeps a plot of ground here for his own family. Living in Ono again, he is close to both the villages of his youth, though Kuba, like Ono, has grown considerably. The hill of the graveyard had to be cut away at the base to make way for a new high school. Growth is natural, Kawamoto says, but he regrets modern disconnections from the past. "Now the future is everything." Still, he believes that the world is in many ways better off than before the war. He is glad in retrospect that the Americans won the war—a feeling expressed by many Japanese his age. Under the military regime, Japan's spirit would have perished, he says. Japan needed democracy, and it took losing the war to achieve it.

He is opposed to the existence of nuclear weapons. Both as the director of the Peace Memorial Museum and as a *hibakusha,* he can speak with authority about nuclear force, but he makes his case briefly and without evident passion. "I am not a philosopher," he says. If pressed as to what he thinks the world will do with nuclear weapons, he admits that he is worried. At the same time he ascribes his own sense of practicality to the world: "Human beings are not fools. We are not likely to destroy everything. We must leave our traditions to the generations."

Mainly he believes in what he saw those August days in 1945. He believes in the piles of bodies in the river and in the melted skin and in the fires in the sky. He believes in Ota. In the present, he believes in his wife and in his home. He would believe in children too, if he had any. But he would not have children; he was afraid they would be affected by possible genetic damage caused by radiation. He believes quite strongly in his house, onto which he has just built an additional room. The house is lovely; it sits on a hill just below his mother's house in Ono. He says that one improves one's house as one improves one's life, and that when you die, you must leave both house and life in as good shape as possible. All this, he explains, is part of the Japanese way of thinking. That all things are transitory, and that their value derives from the fact that they shine brightly before they pass away. For this reason, says Kawamoto, one must keep track of one's experiences.

On Aug. 11, 1945, Yoshitaka Kawamoto sat in the tent in Taibi, half awake in the darkness. Suddenly his mother entered, and the two caught sight of each other. "It was the first time I cried."

-»» II ««-

WHAT
THE PHYSICIST SAW

"No, I wasn't on the *Enola Gay*. I was on the *Great Artiste*, the instrument plane, which measured the yield, the size of the blast. We were right next to the *Enola Gay* when she dropped the Bomb. It was I who got the pictures. I didn't take 'em. Let's say I had a hand in 'em. But I brought the films back. They were on a 16-mm color cassette, and the only processing facility we had out there was for black-and-white movies on reels, so they couldn't process what we had, and we didn't know if anything was on 'em or not. I had to get 'em back to the lab over Groves' dead body. Groves had a policy that everything in the field went to him first, and he tried to get the films away from me. That's a story in itself—cops 'n' robbers. So how do you keep the films from General Groves when you're going from Tinian to Kwajalein to Johnston

Island to Hawaii to San Francisco to Wendover, Utah, to 'Albuquerque, stopping every time with some gumshoe lookin' in the plane and asking, 'Anybody on board by the name of Agnew? He has something I've been ordered by General Groves to *get.* '

"Well, I didn't put [the films] in my brassiere or up my ass, but I *got* 'em. Still, I got caught in Albuquerque. That's when they really closed in on me. But I cut a deal. We'd take the pictures to Oppie, and he'd decide what to do."

Harold M. Agnew's elbows make a pair of wings for his head, on top of which his hands fold in a clasp. The elbows are covered by suede patches sewn onto a brown tweed jacket. The collar of his brown polo shirt is worn over the jacket collar. There is a Western-style belt of silver and turquoise, and something of a belly: the paunch of a man of 64 who was an athlete 40 years ago. He looks like Spencer Tracy now. His desk looks like a pile of raked leaves. On walls and tables in his not-too-large office are honorary university degrees; a photo taken with Attorney General Edwin Meese; another photo taken years ago on Tinian, showing Agnew and his fellow scientists at a briefing session the night before the Hiroshima bombing; and near his desk, a framed photo of his wife Beverly, now 65, looking crisp and very smart in 1939.

These mementos belong to the president of GA Technologies Inc., a company described in its brochure as one of "diverse interests and programs, ranging from the development of advanced energy conversions systems to the production of nuclear instrumentation and radiation monitoring equipment." "They still give me an office to play in," says Agnew, suggesting that his days of hands-on running the company are over. GA Technologies is a very big thing to run: 1984 sales of $160 million and 1,800 employees. Filling 350 well-tended acres behind a high wire gate near La Jolla, Calif., the company resembles a little village, which, instead of a school, a church and a store, consists of a Fusion Building, Waste Yard Buildings and Experimental Area Buildings No. 1, No. 1-Bunker and No. 2.

In fact, GA Technologies looks a good deal like the Los Alamos Scientific Laboratory, of which Agnew was once the director, succeeding Norris Bradbury, who succeeded Los Alamos' first director, J. Robert Oppenheimer, the "Oppie" of the story about the swiped films. The "Groves" is General Leslie Groves, military commander of the Manhattan Project. The films Groves was chasing were the only ones taken of the Hiroshima bomb at the moment it went off. Agnew's *Great Artiste* was one of the planes seen by the boys in Yoshitaka Kawamoto's schoolyard when assembly was held the morning of Aug. 6. It may also have been the B-29 spotted by Kawamoto's classmate Fujimoto when Kawamoto started toward the window for a look.

Agnew was only 24 when he went up in the *Great Artiste*, but he had already seen a lot of the new world of split atoms. As a physics student straight out of college, he was taken by his professor to work with the people at the University of Chicago under Enrico Fermi. At the age of 21, Agnew was one of 43 people to witness the world's first man-made nuclear chain reaction, in a squash court under the football field. A few years later he was testing yield-measuring devices at Wendover Air Base in Utah, where Colonel Paul Tibbets and the atom bomb crew were training in secret. What Agnew saw was much of the history of America's scientific and military progress toward the Hiroshima bombing. He also observed the close relationship that developed between science and the military after the Bomb was dropped. As director of Los Alamos from 1970 to 1979, he later superintended that relationship.

For 40 years, then, Harold Agnew's life tracked the atomic age—from Chicago to Los Alamos to Hiroshima to Los Alamos to La Jolla. His perspective on Hiroshima specifically is that a bomb had to be made and a war won.

Not that any of this history occupies the forefront of Agnew's mind at the moment. These days he is steaming over the IRS, which refuses to give him a tax deduction on those films of Hiroshima. Here is what happened after he cut the deal with Groves:

"I called Oppie ahead of time to explain what was going on. And while we were negotiating, a guy from the lab grabbed the films and went to L.A. with 'em, 'cause that was the only place in the country where they could be processed. It turned out we really struck gold with those pictures. We *got* it. After that we settled the business, and gave copies to Groves. When the war was over, Oppie gave me the originals, and I'd let people use 'em.

"But then Senator [Bob] Packwood heard I had these things, and said they ought to be put in the Smithsonian. So I looked, but I decided that they'd wind up behind some stuffed owl. Then Glenn Campbell of the Hoover Institution [of War, Revolution and Peace at Stanford University] wanted 'em, so I gave 'em to him. A few months later, I got an appraisal from Sotheby's for a deduction on my income tax. Well, since then I've been fighting the IRS. This Wednesday we're having a hearing. Seems they sent the films to Ray Hackie's Film Service. And Ray Hackie's Film Service said the films are worthless. Said they'd been taken with a hand-held camera. There's no script and no score.

"I'm not *kidding*. No script and no *score*. So I have to hire an attorney. It's funny, but it's not so *funny*. That's the IRS for you. Not a thing you can do about it. The way they're going to get their money is through the taxes the lawyer pays 'em after me payin' *him*.

"And another thing I got is the original strike orders [for the bombing], which are rather impressive. They were posted on the bulletin board in Tinian, telling us what planes to use, and when to go to breakfast, and when you take off. And the thing that gets me: you read all the way down—so many gallons of gasoline, and so on—until you get to 'Bomb: Special.' Just said 'Special.' Course, the IRS says that's worthless too. What's a country boy to *do*?"

From time to time the phone rings, and the country boy enters another imminent negotiation. He is trying to sell one of his four cars, a '66 Ford with 208,000 miles on it. Someone has just informed him that the car has a burned-out valve. "You still wanna buy it?"

He addresses the past again. "Did we have to drop the Bomb? You bet your life we did. I wrote an article a couple of years ago recounting my experiences as a member of the U.S. delegation to the United Nations General Assembly Second Session on Disarmament [June 1982]. Outside the U.S. building a group was sitting and marching in silence in memory of Hiroshima. Not Pearl Harbor but Hiroshima. No one seems to realize that without Pearl Harbor there wouldn't have *been* a Hiroshima." He goes back to the beginning:

"The way things really got started was in late '41, after Pearl Harbor. Actually for me, before that time. I was a student at the University of Denver. That's my hometown. And we were all signing up to join the Army Air Corps. Many of my classmates had run off to Canada. That was when you'd run off to Canada to get *into* a war, not stay out of one. In fact, my classmate Keith Johnson got shot down in the Battle of Britain. So we were all signing up. But a professor of mine said, 'Don't sign up in that program. I think something's happening where you can be much more useful.' That's all I knew. A couple of weeks later he said, 'You're going to Chicago.'

"In those days there were only a handful of places in the whole country that knew anything about nuclear energy—nuclear *physics*. It was just in '38 that Enrico Fermi got the Nobel Prize for his work with neutrons, so it was all really brand new. What happened was that the heads of the few places—Ernest Lawrence at Berkeley, Arthur Compton at Chicago, John Dunning at Columbia—they contacted all their former graduates and said, 'Come on back.' They were told that if they knew any semiliterate undergraduates, bring 'em too. It's for the war. So my professor at Denver brought me, first to Columbia, then to Chicago, to see what was going on. Not really. I don't think I knew what was going on as far as the Bomb was concerned for maybe nine months. Anyway, we went to Chicago and started building the first man-made chain reaction.

"I wrote an article about the squash court experiment too—if I can find the goddam thing. I write lots of articles. Course, nobody ever reads 'em." After a minute, he comes up with "Early Recollections of the Manhattan Project," an address to the Society of Nuclear Medicine meeting in Chicago in June 1977. In the article he describes how Fermi and his assistants kept building up the nuclear pile to achieve a critical mass, the smallest amount of material needed to begin a chain reaction. They calculated that on the night between Dec. 1 and Dec. 2, 1942, the 57th layer of graphite would make the pile critical. To prevent the neutrons from multiplying and starting a reaction, the scientists used cadmium strips, which absorb neutrons. When all but one of the cadmium strips were removed, it became clear the calculations were correct. "It was a great temptation for me to partially withdraw the final cadmium strip and to be the first to make a pile chain-react. But Fermi had anticipated this possibility. He had made me promise that I would make the measurement, record the result, insert all cadmium rods, lock them all in place, go to bed, and nothing more.

"What people don't understand is that we were really running frightened of the Germans. The main thing was to get a self-sustaining chain reaction before the Germans did. All the people who were involved—Leo Szilard, John Von Neumann—the whole gaggle of 'em had just got off the boat. Fermi's wife was Jewish. The rest of the guys were Jewish. That's why they left. But all the other Huns, their colleagues, were back home, probably working on a chain reaction. So there was a lot of pressure.

"Well, anyway, we put the stuff together the next morning, and it looked as if the thing was going to go critical. Then Fermi says, 'Let's go have *lunch.*' You'd think he'd want to stay around and finish the damn thing. The criticality kept going up. The counters kept clicking faster and faster. You don't see anything when this happens. The counter just keeps accelerating, like in your car. Course, in a bomb it goes so fast, it blows the thing apart. But then Fermi shuts everything off and says, 'Let's have *lunch.*' So we started it all up again in the afternoon, and it went critical, and that was that.

"Let me tell you, even at this point I still didn't know what the hell this was all about. Everything was very secret. Besides the Hiroshima films and the strike orders, I got a very interesting tape by Fermi talking about secrecy. He points out that things were classified first by the *scientists,* not by the military. You hear things now about how the damn Government classified science; not so. I have the tape. He even hired a guy from Yale to draw up the rules for classification. An absolute paranoid. Excellent choice."

The uneasy relationship between the scientists and the military was beginning to find its shape about the time of the Chicago chain reaction. Only three years earlier Albert Einstein, advised by his fellow refugee physicists Leo Szilard and Eugene P. Wigner that the Germans were likely to

produce an atomic weapon, had addressed a letter to President Roosevelt warning of "extremely powerful bombs of
a new type." Once Roosevelt was persuaded that America
ought to have that bomb first, he set in motion, albeit very
slow motion initially, a coordination of scientific effort
that would lead inevitably to a working partnership with
the American military. Watson Davis, a science editor of
the 1930s, anticipated the central difficulty of that partnership in a single observation: "The most important problem before the scientific world today is not the cure of
cancer, the discovery of a new source of energy, or any
specific achievement. It is: How can science maintain its
freedom and . . . help preserve a peaceful and effective
civilization?"

In a time of war against world-seizing powers, Davis'
question had to lead science logically, purposefully and
enthusiastically toward a collegial relationship with the
American military. Once that relationship was established
it was not to be undone. After Hiroshima, with or without a
war serving as matchmaker, the soldiers and the physicists
were to be wedded for the rest of the century. Yet in the
1940s it was not with the military per se that many scientists believed they were forming a partnership. Rather, it
was with the war as a specific and isolated entity. Agnew recalls how zealously Oppenheimer worked to keep the scientists in a draft-free status: an effort for symbolic, if not
functional, independence.

For their part, most of the military had no knowledge
of the atom bomb project. General Groves was in charge
of the Manhattan Project at Los Alamos and on Tinian, but

he served as a manager and coordinating supervisor—an exceptionally capable one, according to Agnew; an overbearing and tyrannical one, according to critics—not as a commander directly involved with the conduct of the war. Not even General Douglas MacArthur, the monarchical commander in the Pacific, knew of the Bomb in the making.

Yet while these two technically separate units of physicists and soldiers trained and worked in relative isolation from each other for an event no one was sure would ever take place, and while the scientists restricted their intellectual freedom in pursuit of preserving their civic freedom, the fact is that both they and the military were working their way toward the same meeting place. That their relationship would be sealed over Hiroshima deeply troubled some of the scientists afterward, who may have read in the aerial pairing of the *Enola Gay* and the *Great Artiste* the end of their control over a universe they had disclosed. In 1943, however, most of the scientists wanted victory first, and Los Alamos was their theater.

"You want to know how I got to Los Alamos? It was my wife's good looks. We were married in May 1942, and Beverly got a job as personal secretary to R.L. Doan, the administrative head of the project in Chicago. She also handled the whole security system in Chicago—21 years old, an English *literature* major. She was pretty too, and whenever Oppie came around, he liked to talk to her. Naturally, when Oppie was going to start up the lab in Los Alamos, he decided that he needed someone to work for him who had experience—like Beverly. So he asked her to come to

New Mexico. And it was reasonable that I should go too. Fact is, it seemed that everyone and everything was going to Los Alamos. The Princeton guys, the Illinois people. *Tremendous* effort. People today don't appreciate how frightened we were. Things were really going down the tube in '41, '42, '43. We were losing badly in the Pacific. There was Bataan. Hong Kong fell Christmas Day. The Atlantic was just horrendous.

"Anyway, when I showed up at Los Alamos, it was a Sunday, and my wife hadn't arrived yet, 'cause she was home saying goodbye to her brother, who was off to the war. And I ran into Oppie. And all he said was: 'Where's Beverly?' Which crushed me. From that day I knew exactly where I stood with *that* guy." Agnew chuckles. "I never really liked the guy, anyway. He was too smart and too rich and too handsome.

"And he was really a smoothie. We got about 128 bucks a month. The plumbers at Los Alamos were getting between $500 and $750. And the plumbers couldn't do anything the physicists couldn't do. So we went to see Oppie, about six of us, and complained. And Oppie says, 'The difference is that you know what you're doin' and the plumbers don't.' Then he walks out. And we *took* it. What an operator."

Modern Los Alamos makes it easy to picture what the town looked like in 1943, when the physicists began to arrive and settle in. Like Hiroshima, Los Alamos lives in two eras simultaneously; a road sign near Bandelier National Monument park indicates six miles to the "Atomic City. Birthplace of the Atomic Age, scientific laboratory and museum, gas-food-lodging-golf course." The makeshift wooden apartments that once housed the physicists and their families are long down, as are the PX with its cathedral-like jukebox and the commissary and the walls of bed sheets drying in the sun in front of Quonset huts. Yet photographs of all these are retained and displayed prominently in the new buildings, whose functions differ from the originals only in scope. The main business of Los Alamos is what it has been since the town popped up on a plateau just east of the continental divide 42 years ago: the design and development of nuclear weapons. These functions are performed in a surrounding of caves, canyons, mesas, mountains and sky so beautiful that all one has to do is look up from his work for a moment, and the day has changed.

"We came to this wonderful world," said Nobel Prizewinner I.I. Rabi in a speech at Los Alamos a few years ago when the alumni reconvened. Rabi's speech was double-edged. Titled "How Well We Meant," it both recalled the necessity of nuclear weapons and lamented their subsequent expansion. But in the beginning "it happened to be one of those spring days where everything was lovely. The air was clear and mild, the Sangre de Cristo Mountains were distinct and sharp, the mesa on the other side—lovely! And the ride up on the old road, somewhat hair raising but very interesting, the old bridge, and then, of course, the Indians; we certainly seemed to enter a new world, a mystic world."

Both the mystic and the real world are exhibited in the Bradbury Science Museum. It is about the size of Kawamoto's Peace Museum, and it too tells the story of an event and its consequences. Exhibits are arranged to indicate causalities. Einstein's letter to F.D.R. is located on a wall below a newspaper headline of the times: GERMANY ANNEXES AUSTRIA. There is a letter from Groves to Oppenheimer, requesting that Oppenheimer avoid flying in airplanes: "The time saved is not worth the risk." A photograph shows the July 16, 1945, Trinity test explosion at Alamogordo, looking like a glazed white coffee cup overturned on a bed of suds.

Oddest among the exhibits are two life-size, life-shape, white plaster models of Groves and Oppenheimer: the one, thick-fleshed in an oversize Army uniform, the cast accurate to the bulge in Groves' breast pocket, perhaps made by the chocolates to which he reportedly was addicted; the other skinny, stooped, in an unpressed civilian suit and floppy hat. From hats to shoes, all white, the two of them. All white, too, is a model of "Little Boy" lying on the floor—120 in. long, 28 in. in diameter, nearly 9,000 lbs.— looking like a small, friendly Moby Dick. Another striking figure in the museum is that of "Plastic Man," described as "one of the most popular of all the laboratory's residents during the 1950s." The transparent dummy was used to test levels of radiation on human beings after an atomic blast.

The main event in the museum is a film called *The Town That Never Was,* shown on a regular schedule in a small theater where the seats are carpeted rises. Hiroshima is never mentioned in this film, which for some reason begins with voices in prayer in church and the figure of Jesus covered with blood. Then the film proceeds to show the Chicago squash court and herky-jerky conversations among Szilard, Wigner, Edward Teller and the rest. A jalopy convertible winds up a mountain road in a scene that might have come from a Gene Autry western of the 1930s. There are sudden shots of the Statue of Liberty; sheep and golden flowers by a roadside; the Los Alamos Ranch School, which occupied the land before the lab came, a place where wealthy families sent sickly boys for toughening. The film's narrator says that "Indians willingly relinquished land for the sake of the war," and he describes the uniqueness of Los Alamos in terms of negatives: "No invalids, no idle rich, no in-laws, no unemployed, no jails, no sidewalks, no garages, no paved roads." The film ends with sailors bussing girls on the streets of New York, and references to the future of nuclear energy and "rockets to the stars."

When Agnew arrived at Los Alamos in March 1943, there were no invalids, no idle rich, no paved roads and not much room.

"Beverly and I shared a bunkhouse with one other couple and a fella from the University of Nebraska, a guy named Jorgensen, who would eat only Chinese food. He elected himself cook. We ate Chinese food three times a day, Chinese oatmeal for breakfast. He cooked on a hot plate and slept in the hall, while the two couples had one small bedroom each. But it worked great. I loved the place. Easterners had a time getting used to all this primitive discomfort, but I was in hog heaven. It was also a completely democratic society. Oppie saw to that—big shots and flun-

kies like me all living together. Every week we had a collo-
quium in one of our two movie theaters, where we would
be told what everyone was doing. Once in a while some
military guy would come by and give us a pep talk.

"Soon as we got there our job was to put together an
accelerator, which was brought from the University of Illinois in Champaign. A team of us—Bernie Waldman from
Notre Dame and John Manley, who'd come from Illinois
and Columbia, and people from Nebraska and Wiscon-
sin—we all pitched in. We worked six days a week to get
the Bomb first. There's been a lot of stories that maybe we
had the Bomb and were sitting on it, that we could have
used it in Germany but because we're Anglo-Saxons or
whatever, that we only went against the Asians. That's not
true. As soon as we got the Bomb we were ready to drop it.

"First we had to figure out how the thing would be designed. Everyone was working just as fast as possible—either on the gun-assembly method, which was used for the
uranium bomb in Hiroshima, or on the implosion method,
which we used for the plutonium bomb at Trinity and later
in Nagasaki. [George] Kistiakowsky pooh-poohed the implosion idea at first; he was a real tough cookie. But then
he got behind it. Both bombs were going ahead full
steam."

As it turned out, the Hiroshima bomb would be the
only one of its type America ever built or used, uranium
being that much more difficult to obtain than plutonium.
One of the spurs to the American atom bomb effort had
been a report in 1943 that Hitler had ordered uranium
shipped out of mines in Belgium. It was also taken for

granted that the gun-assembly method—one piece of pu-
rified uranium (uranium-235) fired into another at terrific
speed—would work, so the Hiroshima bomb was never
tested till the morning it was dropped.

While the people in Los Alamos were working to produce their bomb, physicists in Japan were attempting to
produce theirs. Professor Hidetake Kakihana of Sophia
University in Tokyo was Agnew's age when he too was en-
listed by his country in 1941 to assist with nuclear fission
experiments at a secret cyclotron in Tokyo under the directorship of Yoshio Nishina, Japan's Oppenheimer. Unlike Agnew, Kakihana and many of his colleagues were re-
luctant to produce an atom bomb for their government
because they had great distaste for the military regime.
The physicists worked, Kakihana says today, with deliberate slowness.

If Japan's military regime really wanted to produce an
atom bomb before the Americans, it put almost no money
behind the effort, compared with the Americans' $2 bil-
lion. For their part, the Japanese physicists simply made
the wrong scientific choice in their fission experiments,
deciding to work with high-energy rather than low-energy
neutrons. Even if they had been able to produce a chain reaction, there was very little uranium in the country and no
way to get more. There is little doubt that if the Japanese
had made a Bomb before the Americans, they would have
used it, but the question is moot. Kakihana always believed
that the U.S. would build the Bomb first, but he thought
that the Americans would use it only in a demonstration.

"All the while," Agnew says, "I really was aching to get

in the war. Pure and simple. I wanted in especially because all my classmates and my friends in Denver were in. We had an all-city softball team. My catcher got killed in the war—a guy named Howard Erikson. And all the other kids—Bob Hogan, who would have made, maybe, an All-America golf and/or football player, he got killed. *Everybody* was gettin' killed. Or they were off fighting someplace. And of course, the neighbors wanted to know where *I* was. And my parents said they really didn't know, but they knew I was doin' *something*. Well, it sounded as if I'd gone over the hill. That really bothered me. And it bothered them, but they really didn't know where we were. We had a P.O. box, that's all. So I wanted in. If I was ever asked, 'What did you do in the war, Daddy?' I could say, 'I did *this*. I didn't hide under a *bush*.'

"Luckily for me, in late '44 [fellow Physicist] Luis Alvarez, who also wanted to get in the war, came up with the idea that we were neglecting our responsibilities if we didn't try to measure the yield of the Bomb while we were making it. Well, as soon as I heard about this, I went and pounded on Luis' door and said I wanted to play, and I became a member of his team. I knew that if I could handle measuring the yield, that I'd be going overseas. So did Luis. We knew too that we would get to fly on missions We'd be as important as a tail gunner, even one who never fired a shot."

Today Agnew is glad to see a mutual understanding between the soldiers and the physicists. He is annoyed by those of his former colleagues at Los Alamos who believe that science struck a perilous bargain with the military during the war. That was the thrust of Rabi's reunion speech: "We gave away the power to people who didn't understand it and were not grown up enough and responsible enough to realize what they had." Rabi's speech "really irritated me," says Agnew, who was at that same reunion and whose own speech declared that the Japanese "bloody well deserved" what they got. "I have always felt that science and the military *should* work together. And they *have*, from Day One, whether it was Leonardo da Vinci or Michelangelo or whoever. They were always designing things for the people in charge."

Other physicists, agreeing with Rabi, take the view that the military-scientific partnership was not only dangerous to the country but detrimental to the quality of American science as well. Philip Morrison, celebrated for his teaching at the Massachusetts Institute of Technology, carried the container of plutonium in his hands from Los Alamos to the Trinity test site and, like Agnew, was on Tinian the days of the bombings. Now he spends a good part of his intellectual life arguing for disarmament. Morrison also felt that the Bomb was needed to end the war. Looking back today, however, he says that the physicists learned something after they transferred "their science directly from the peaceable study of the ultimate structure of matter to the fearful desolation of Hiroshima . . . They learned rather quickly what had to be done next if we are able to survive for a long time. The statesmen have not learned so quickly, but it is true that their task is a much harder one."

After Hiroshima and Nagasaki, Morrison's main concern was "how to get the Bomb into the *peace*." But once

THE WORLD SINCE HIROSHIMA

World War II was over, American scientists were inevitably associated in the public mind with war. Hiroshima had entirely changed the popular image of the unworldly professor; he had proved what he could *do*. By the end of the 1940s, the Soviets had their own atomic weapon, and by 1953, less than a year after the U.S., they tested their first hydrogen bomb. Once the arms race was a fact, the U.S. seemed to need its physicists as saviors and protectors. Places like Los Alamos were transformed from emergency-inspired experimental labs to permanent national institutions. People like Oppenheimer and Morrison left Los Alamos to return to their universities as soon as the war was done. People like Agnew stayed on.

At Los Alamos today, Merri Wood, a tall brunet with a bright, clear-liquid voice and a designer of nuclear weapons, is in a sense Agnew's heir and creation. Not only does Wood not question the connection of her work with the military, she is pleased to have it. For one thing, that connection has provided jobs for those like herself, a former Ph.D. candidate in physics at Georgia Tech, who was specializing in particle transport and found a shop to apply her studies. (Particle transport is a general term for the motion of atomic particles through various materials.) Designing weapons is something Wood wanted to do since junior high school, when she read "everything I could lay my hands on" about the men making the first Bomb. "Out of patriotism, maybe glamour, I don't know, I really admired those people. I never dreamed that I'd be doing it. I'm tickled pink."

As a day-to-day matter, Wood has to think about the

military, since the military, by making requests and assignments, gives direction to her work in "thermonuclear applications" (designing warheads). "The military wants XYZ bomb, and you give 'em the best you can." She tests a bomb's size and, like Agnew before her, measures yield. "If they [the military] say they want two megatons, I give 'em two; if they want 2,000, I give 'em 2,000." The measure of success is if a bomb tests satisfactorily in Nevada and then goes into stockpile. In that case Wood works with the engineer on the final design of the weapon—"weaponize is the term." A bomb must be "buildable, reliable and robust. If one little thing jiggles, it can't quit working." Design is as far as she goes. "You design it, you field it, you sit there with sweaty palms and wait for the ground to shake."

Wood enjoys the connection between her work and its military market because she sees a philosophical underpinning. The people at Los Alamos when Agnew was there were working toward something they knew was going to be used. The people at Los Alamos now work on things that are never supposed to be used. "And we don't want to use them. *Nobody* wants to see these guys used." Nor does she feel that there is something antilogical or frustrating in designing a weapon for the explicit purpose of not using it The "in-point," she says, is in the test or in the stockpile. "We have a fellow here who hangs a peace sign from his badge.

"Now we joke: let's nuke Tehran. But we're human beings. We live here with families. We want a good national defense, and most people believe that a nuclear deterrent is the way to go. For that reason we get satisfaction from our work by contributing to our personal and national safety. It's corny—wave the flag—but it's true." As for those who dropped the Hiroshima bomb, she says that guilt or conscience ought not to be the consideration. "If a policeman shoots a felon, there's no guilt, only regret. You just wish the world had been different."

Agnew favors the military-scientific partnership for another reason. War, he says, is "too important to be left to the young." By which he means that the existence of nuclear weapons is to be approved of because those weapons have put the politicians and generals of a nation, who arrange and orchestrate wars, at equal risk with the young people who do the actual fighting. Science has thus served as an equalizer between leaders and troops: "The young people who go around yelling 'Get rid of the Bomb!' ought to be careful, 'cause the politicians might put a bow and arrow in their hands and make the kids sally forth again, knowing that nothing is going to happen to *them* [the politicians]. With the development of nuclear weapons, the guy who says 'Go fight a war' is talking to him*self.*

"You know what I'd do to keep the world out of a nuclear war? Most of the decision makers have never seen a bomb. These guys talk about bombs—so many kilotons, so many megatons—it doesn't *mean* anything to 'em. So I say maybe every five years every world leader should have to strip down—Mrs. Thatcher in her bikini and the other guys in skivvies—and watch a multimegaton bomb go off. What'll impress them is not the flash, not the size of the cloud and not the boom. It's the *heat.* If they're about 25 miles away, they will get very antsy, 'cause they'll get hotter and hotter, and they will worry that maybe somebody's made a mistake. The heat. Really scares the bejesus out of you. After that the chances of their ever using a bomb would diminish *rapidly.*"

He also makes it clear that he is less opposed to the proponents of disarmament than to an attitude that suggests that in the real world the U.S. has no right or reason to maintain nuclear weapons, and, for that matter, that the Americans had no business bombing Hiroshima in the first place. "A few years ago, Senator [Mark] Hatfield organized a big peace exhibit in the rotunda of the Senate. So here's this big exhibit, and all it showed was the horrors of Hiroshima. [Some of the artifacts came from the Hiroshima Peace Museum.] All the burned victims. Just awful things. Melted cups. Now my objection was that in a *peace* exhibit you ought to have shown Pearl Harbor too. Then you could say, 'This is the way it started, and this is the way it ended. Let's not do this again.' "

One more phone call about the Ford. Eventually he sells it for $200. Says the *tires* are worth *that.*

"So anyway, I finally got to go to Tinian, flying from Los Alamos to San Francisco to Hawaii to Johnston Island. In Hawaii you would see where the American ships were sunk—parts of 'em sticking out of the water. And you'd see the pockmarks on the buildings. And when you got to Johnston Island, there were wrecked planes on the field. And when you got to Kwajalein, there'd been one *hell* of a battle there. I picked spent bullets right off the ground— .30 caliber, .50 caliber. Parts of airplanes and amphibious vehicles lay all over the place. The control tower was all busted up. Then we got to Tinian, and all the Japanese buildings were gutted. Remnants, standing like Coventry. You went around to these places, and you got the idea that *something* had been going on.

"I got to Tinian in March 1945, and the *Indianapolis* arrived in July with the uranium from Los Alamos. The *Indianapolis* was sunk by the Japanese after it left Tinian; if it had been hit before, no Hiroshima. We were working six days a week on Tinian, trying to get ready for the mission. We all got jungle rot on our feet and hands. I remember going to a doctor and asking what to do. He told me, 'Scratch it.' I used to watch the B-29s, hundreds of 'em, coming back from missions like a flock of geese. Those big airplanes, coming in to land. Some smoking, some with their props feathered."

One thing Agnew and Philip Morrison do agree on: when you went to the movies on Tinian you could not hear the sound track for the rain beating on your helmet. Morrison remembers them always playing a follow-the-bouncing-ball sing-along of *White Christmas*—the G.I.s bellowing *White Christmas* all spring and summer. He also remembers the physicists preparing the necessary ingredients for ice cream, then sending the concoction up 30,000 ft. in a B-29 to freeze the stuff: a $25,000 dessert. And he remembers the bombers going on missions before Aug. 6. Sometimes the planes would be overloaded and would crash on takeoff. Great pillars of fire would rise on the beach, men burning alive inside them.

Of the original four runways on Tinian, two are still operable: wide, white, gleaming strips made of coral and as-

phalt, surrounded by orange flame trees bent by the mild
wind toward the ocean, and green spongy hills, and the en-
croaching thick, tall grass. The island is nearly empty now,
down from a population of 20,000 U.S. servicemen in
1945 to 800 Chamorro natives, who fish, raise goats or
herd cattle. Not far from the runways stands the bombed-
out shell of the Japanese officers' quarters: charred tim-
bers, a huge bomb hole in the roof, a tree blooming
through the hole. Not far from there is what looks like a
fresh grave, about 10 ft. by 18 ft., in a grassed-over area
that once was "Atomic Bomb Pit No. 1," marked by a sign
that resembles a picnic-area sign in a public park. Growing
on the plot are a dwarfed and twisted coconut tree and a
pometia tree that looks like a stalk of grapes stripped bare.
Before the plot is a stone marker shaped like a public trash
can with an inscription saying that here the Bomb was
loaded up into the *Enola Gay* on the afternoon of Aug. 5. It
was Agnew's day.

"And then came the night of our mission. Our B-29s
had a circle with a black arrow in it as their insignia. All the
other B-29s had triangles or circles with letters of the al-
phabet. But the night before the mission, on Aug. 5, Tokyo Rose came on the radio and said, 'Black Arrow Squad-
ron, we know who you are and what you are, and we are
ready for you.' Early the next morning we didn't have
black arrows anymore. We had triangles with letters,
which I thought was chicken. But it was prudent.

"So off we went, flying near the *Enola Gay* all the way,
all 13 hours. The weather plane had returned and report-
ed that everything was peachy keen. A little before 8:15,

the area was clear, the *Enola Gay* was right on target, and we were alongside, about a quarter-mile away. Then we caught the tone signal, which meant that the Bomb was armed and ready to drop. When the tone went off, that meant the Bomb was on the way down, so we dropped our measuring gauges, our own little 'bombs.' Then we saw the flash of light. And the camera was rolling. We must have been seven miles away when the shock waves hit the plane. All I remember is we sure got out of there in a hurry, which was fine by me. I just wanted to get home."

⇛ III ⇚

WHAT
THE PRESIDENT SAW

On July 4, 1985, Richard Nixon sits in a low-back armchair, his legs crossed on an ottoman, his hands contributing to his account of the past 40 years of atomic diplomacy by drawing circles in the air, playing an absent piano, shooing away a wrong idea, coming together in an arch or making points in precise order: one, two, three, four. It is shortly after 8 a.m. Two mornings back to back he has been discussing the effects of Hiroshima on the world and on the presidency in his office in a federal building in downtown Manhattan. The building's air-conditioning system is off because of the national holiday, but the room is not yet hot. Outside, the streets are empty and lifeless, except for a McDonald's. Nixon wears a blue-gray suit, a white shirt and a red-and-white-striped tie. The chair he occupies is backed into a corner of the office.

Wide windows on either side of him offer a view of anti-
quated wooden water tanks on the rooftops of nearby
buildings and a sky that is pale blue and still as a wall.

"Oh yes, I remember vividly. I was in New York City
when the Bomb fell. I had returned from the South Pacific
and was stationed at the Bureau of Aeronautics, 50 Church
Street, doing legal work on military contracts. I remember
very clearly that I was going home that night in the subway,
and I saw a newspaper with a headline. Something like MAS-
SIVE BOMB DROPPED ON JAPAN. I didn't give it much thought
because we had heard about the buzz bombs in London
and the other new weapons that were used during the war,
and I said, well, this is just another one. I just assumed the
war would go on.

"So I was surprised when V-J day came a week later. I
really hadn't celebrated V-E day very much because I knew
how tough the Japanese were, and that the war in the Pacific might take a long time. I was sure that I would be rotated
back to duty on one of the islands. What I remember about
V-J day is that Mrs. Nixon and I went to Times Square to
celebrate, and I got my pocket picked. Never forget that!
In those days we didn't have a great deal of money. Sort of
put a damper on the day."

The summer of 1945 may have been the last time in his
life that Nixon had the luxury of paying casual attention to
the Bomb. Nuclear weapons were to color politics from
that time on, and Nixon's political career was to extend
from Congress in 1947, to the Senate in 1951, to the vice
presidency under Dwight Eisenhower from 1953 to 1961,
to the presidency in 1969 and again in 1973. His view of

Hiroshima is that the bombing not only brought nuclear weapons into international diplomacy but that it brought America into the world. What he saw in Hiroshima was the beginning of national stature on a global scale, the onset of American maturity.

"Should the Bomb have been used against Japan? There's no simple answer. [General Douglas] MacArthur once spoke to me very eloquently about it, pacing the floor of his apartment in the Waldorf. He thought it a tragedy that the Bomb was ever exploded. MacArthur believed that the same restrictions ought to apply to atomic weapons as to conventional weapons, that the military objective should always be limited damage to noncombatants.

"Now we have to put that in context. If that proposition had been accepted during the war generally, the Allies would not have bombed Germany, and we would not have made earlier strikes against Japan. Remember, at least 35,000 were killed in one night in Dresden. Our fire bombing of Tokyo [in March 1945] killed 83,000 in a single night. They all were deliberate bombings of civilian areas. MacArthur, you see, was a soldier. He believed in using force only against military targets, and that is why the nuclear thing turned him off, which I think speaks well of him.

"But looking at it another way, in terms of whether or not the bombing of Hiroshima saved lives in the long run, most observers agree that it did. If we had invaded the main islands, it would have cost perhaps a million American casualties, certainly more than a million Japanese. How many civilian deaths did the nuclear bomb cause?

Well, it cost a total of 200,000 in two places, and that's terrible. But it may have saved ten times that number.

"Of course the Bomb had a traumatic effect on the Japanese. I was in Hiroshima in the 1960s, speaking at a dinner of the country's leaders. The Japanese are excellent hosts. They drink pretty good, as we say. All through my speech there was clapping and laughing, and then I mentioned the bombing, something to the effect that it should never happen again—and the light went out of their eyes. All the smiles went. It was as if somebody had [he makes the gesture of cutting the air with a sword]. Like that. Hiroshima was simply too horrible to think about."

In saying that the Hiroshima bombing saved ten times as many lives as it claimed, Nixon may actually be understating the issue. In fact, estimates at the time were that as many as 10 million Japanese would have been lost in an American invasion, as well as a million U.S. troops. In the summer of 1945, Japan had more than 2 million soldiers and 30 million citizens prepared to choose death over dishonor. The kamikaze pilots and the Japanese troops who fought at Okinawa and Iwo Jima had already established the point. This is not just the American view. Kawamoto and most other Japanese today feel that Japan's military government never would have surrendered without an absolute catastrophe.

Whether or not America used the atom bomb solely to effect that surrender is another question. After Europe, the nation had its bellyful of war, and the assumption of the times was if the Bomb could bring peace in one shot, then use the thing. But a strong impulse for retribution must have applied as well. Harold Agnew was not alone in feeling that the Japanese "bloody well deserved" Hiroshima. There is also a theory that the U.S. used the Bomb as much to frighten the Soviets, with whom it was about to divide the world, as to win the war with Japan. More have dismissed this theory than embraced it. The Soviets, however, believe it to this day.

Then, too: Was it in fact the Bomb that brought the war to an end? The Japanese government was in total disarray in the summer of 1945, so Hiroshima and Nagasaki may merely have provided an excuse for a surrender. The Soviets entered the war on Aug. 8—after Hiroshima and before Nagasaki. The Japanese may have concluded that it would be better to surrender to the Americans than to risk prolonging the war and allowing the Soviets to take more spoils. The U.S. Strategic Bombing Survey conducted just after the war concluded that the atom bombings were not decisive in defeating the Japanese, and in reality may have strengthened their will to resist.

Certainly almost all who were involved in the Hiroshima decision believed at the time that the Bomb would be effective and that its use was necessary. Both presumptions, applied initially to Japan, were soon to shape all nuclear diplomacy after the war, since the presumptions of necessity and effectiveness would make threats to use nuclear weapons believable. Nixon inherited those presumptions, though he came to question them. He did not believe that the bombing of civilian populations wins wars. Eventually the whole problem was to be made immaterial, once Soviet and American nuclear weapons so grew in numbers and in power that the threat of mutual annihilation emerged as the only strategy available to either side. At first Nixon observed this process. Later he managed it.

"I didn't really begin to realize the significance of the Bomb until I was a candidate for Congress, and came to Washington in 1947. Even then, my sense of how the Bomb changed the geopolitical balance of the world grew rather gradually. There were two immediate developments as a result of our having the Bomb. One: the demobilization on the part of the U.S.—much too fast. Two: the demobilization on the parts of the British and the French—much too fast because they had the crutch of the Bomb. Suddenly the U.S. was the most powerful nation in the world. From that time forward, whether we wanted to or not, we would have to play a major role on the world's stage.

"And I would say that we did *not* want to play that role. World power is something very much opposed to the ingrained American attitude. Basically, Americans are idealists. We go into war for pragmatic reasons, but we have to be appealed to on idealistic terms. We are very impatient about being in a world where balance of power may make a difference, where one must sometimes recognize that you win without getting total victory. The fact that the Bomb made us a world power meant that we had to learn how to be one, and it has been very difficult."

As Nixon talks, the mannerisms for which he has often been burlesqued start to crop up. Yet in his presence the sudden scowl, the self-administered hug are not only not funny; they do not seem at all spasmodic or out of joint with what he is saying. He is 72, and perhaps his manner-isms have grown less pronounced over the years. But here he is speaking about things with which he feels supremely comfortable, history and diplomacy, and the comfort shows in his face and body.

At the same time, he is plainly not comfortable talking to a stranger, and that shows too. Occasional informalities are quickly caught up, crumpled and tossed away. He shows no signs whatever of seeking affection, as one does in a normal conversation, and rather than expanding on an idea or a story in the interests of courtesy, he will begin to fade off, and suddenly snap to attention by saying, "So much for that." There is almost no small talk. The amiabil-ity is reserved for his subject.

"Now let's talk about the Russians. Americans were surprised when the Russians got the Bomb [1949]. So now we both had the Bomb, but the Americans had more of them, and that is when the U.S. started using the Bomb as a diplomatic stick. There is a revisionist theory going around today that the Bomb did not play a significant role in our foreign diplomacy since World War II. The theory has developed because the Bomb is very unpopular. But I *know* it played a role. It played a role in Korea. It played a decisive role in the 1956 crisis in Suez, in calling Khru-shchev's bluff and keeping him out of that area. It also played a decisive role in 1959 in Berlin, when Khrushchev was threatening to pull out of the Four-Power pact. It played a role in Cuba, of course, but a different kind of role, because that was when everything, including the presidency, changed. I'll come to that."

In an article, *The Unimpressive Record of Atomic Diplomacy,* McGeorge Bundy, who was John F. Kennedy's National Security Adviser, takes a somewhat different tack. Arguing that "there is very little evidence that American atomic supremacy was helpful in American diplomacy," Bundy cites Iran in 1946 and Quemoy and Matsu in 1955 and 1958. But he also suggests that atomic diplomacy did not affect the outcome of Korea either. Nixon says otherwise.

"Eisenhower had to find a way to bring that war to a conclusion. The truce talks had gone on for two years. During the talking at Panmunjom, tens of thousands of people were being killed. He had said, 'I will go to Korea,' in our campaign, and he was one of those new politicians who believed he had to keep a promise. Mark Clark was in command. Clark, knowing that Eisenhower did not want to get involved in an expanded ground war in Korea, understood that the only option for breaking the logjam was nuclear weapons.

"Eisenhower probably considered it, but he was concerned about using the Bomb in Korea because it was another Asian country. That had to be in the back of his mind. It was in the back of my mind, at least. And yet he was between a rock and a hard place. He had to end the war, he ruled out the use of ground troops, and all he had was the nuclear option.

"He decided then to give [Secretary of State John Foster] Dulles the responsibility of talking to Krishna Menon, the Indian Ambassador to the United Nations, who had very good relations with both the Russians and the Chinese, and who loved to talk to people—a great blah blah blah. And Dulles—not exactly in a threatening way—said, 'You know, we are very concerned about Korea,' and 'The President's patience is wearing thin,' and finally saying that unless the logjam is broken, it will lead to the use of nuclear weapons. It worked. The Chinese were probably tired of the war. And the Russians did not want to go to war over Korea. But it was the Bomb that did it. I'll tel: you why."

He enumerates what he considers the requirements for successful nuclear diplomacy. The fingers start counting again:

"One, the U.S. must have unquestioned superiority. Two, the place involved in the conflict must be of supreme American interest. Three, a conventional option must not be available. Four—and this may be the biggest factor— the President of the U.S. must have credibility. Korea fit in all respects. But the main thing was that the Russians did not want to mess with Eisenhower. Lyndon Johnson made this point rather sadly once when I had breakfast with him in 1969. He was talking about the bad advice he got about halting the bombing in Viet Nam. He said that Averell Harriman came to him at least twelve times, and said that if we'd stop the bombing, the Russians would use their influence to restrain the North Vietnamese. Johnson said, 'I did it twelve times, and not a one of them did a damn bit of good. Ike was different,' he said. 'The Russians feared Ike. They didn't fear me.' "

Nixon pauses. He seems amazed by Johnson's confession even now. Throughout this whole discussion of the

Bomb's history, he does not move or fidget much, but his voice suggests how involved he is in these recollections.

"In 1956 we considered using the Bomb in Suez, and we did use it diplomatically. The Russians called on us to join them in sending a combined force to drive the British and French out of the area. Eisenhower's response was that that was unthinkable. We were trying to use diplomatic leverage, but he wasn't about to join the Russians against our allies. Well, Khrushchev was feeling his oats, and he made a bloodcurdling threat that the Russians would go in unilaterally. Eisenhower's response was very interesting. He got Al Gruenther, the NATO commander, to hold a press conference, and Gruenther said that if Khrushchev carried out his threat to use rockets against the British Isles, Moscow would be destroyed 'as surely as day follows night.' From that time on, the U.S. has played the dominant role in the Mideast.

"Then there was Berlin." Nixon sits up straight. He is about to tell a story he enjoys.

In 1959 the Soviets were threatening to recognize the East German regime's authority over Berlin, which would have had the effect of denying access to the city for the U.S., France and Britain. It also placed the Adenauer government in jeopardy. Eisenhower made it clear that he would oppose the Soviets' attempt to violate the Four-Power agreement.

"He held a press conference, March 11, 1959. It was Eisenhower at his best. He rambled and rambled. People said he didn't know what he meant. But Eisenhower always rambled deliberately, because he was trying to make a point another way. At the press conference it was mentioned that a new budget had gone up to the Pentagon, reducing American ground forces by 50,000. So one of the first questions shot out of the box by a reporter was if the President, in view of this crisis in Berlin, intended to reevaluate the cutback.

"Eisenhower made one flat statement. He said, 'We are certainly not going to fight a ground war in Europe.' But then he went on to say, 'What possible good would it do to send a few thousand more Americans to Berlin, even a few divisions? After all, there are 500,000 Soviet and German troops in East Germany and 175 Soviet divisions in that neighborhood.' [Nixon repeats "in that neighborhood" with relish.] Somebody brought up *nuclear weapons.* Eisenhower then went off on a monologue about how senseless nuclear war was. He didn't see how nuclear weapons could free *anything.* He gave the impression they were so destructive, so *terrible.* Naive readers of the transcript of that press conference will think that Eisenhower was ruling the Bomb out, because it was so terrible. At the end of the conference, someone raised the nuclear question again, and Eisenhower just closed the conference by saying the United States will stand by its commitments. 'We will do what is necessary to protect ourselves.'

"People asked, 'What in the world are we *doing?* [Nixon feigns bafflement.] We're not going to send in ground forces. Eisenhower speaks disparagingly of the possibility of using nuclear weapons. What does it all *mean?*' Four days later, testimony before a Senate subcommittee by Air Force General Chief of Staff [Thomas] White was released.

White told the Senators that the Berlin crisis could lead to a general war with the Soviet Union and 'nuclear weapons have to be used.' [Nixon relaxes, delighted.] The Russians back down."

He notes that Berlin met all the conditions of successful nuclear diplomacy. He draws a comparison to the Berlin crisis of 1961, which resulted in the building of the Berlin Wall: "Khrushchev backed down with Eisenhower, and went forward with Kennedy." He attempts to emphasize that he is not criticizing the way Kennedy handled the 1961 situation, but then he points out that Kennedy capitalized on the term missile gap in the 1960 campaign, in which he defeated Nixon. "Maybe Khrushchev believed it." Nixon adds that there was no missile gap in 1960. "We actually had a 15-to-1 advantage in strategic missiles at the time of the '62 Cuban missile confrontation. But the 'missile gap' phrase got people worried. Americans are sitting fat and happy on the ultimate weapon, and suddenly they think, well, maybe it isn't always going to be that way."

On the Cuban missile "complication," he focuses on the abilities of Khrushchev, with whom Nixon was linked in the public mind since the publicized "kitchen debate" at the American Exhibition in Moscow in 1959. He rates Khrushchev "the most brilliant world leader I have ever met." That brilliance was manifested, he says, in Khrushchev's having nurtured a reputation for rashness and unpredictability. "He scared the hell out of people." Yet he was the kind of leader, Nixon believes, with whom nuclear weapons were relatively safe—unlike "a nut like Gaddafi." As for those who now say that America's nuclear superiority in 1962 had nothing to do with Khrushchev's backing down, "Don't kid yourself."

But this time nuclear diplomacy worked both ways, he says. Khrushchev backed down, but Kennedy agreed to take U.S. missiles out of Turkey. He also agreed to "quit supporting anti-Castro forces stationed in the United States." Now, according to Nixon, the usefulness of the fear of nuclear retaliation was beginning to wear thin.

"The Cuban missile confrontation was the whole watershed. The Soviet Deputy Foreign Minister [Vasili] Kuznetsov told John McCloy, who had been Kennedy's disarmament adviser, 'We agreed to pull out, but you Americans will never be able to do this to us again.'" After that began the massive Soviet buildup of nuclear arms. "We had a policy of building 1,000 weapons, and we thought that if they built up to 1,000 as well, that would be all right, a standoff. What happened is that they didn't stop at 1,000. That is the situation that confronted me when I became President."

The world of real missiles that Nixon conjures up is one he has never visited. Some of that world lies in Montana, where 200 Minuteman missiles are planted in 23,000 sq. mi. of flat farmland extending from the middle of the state to the northern Rockies. Spread out at good distances from one another are 150 Minuteman IIs and 50 Minuteman IIIs, representing 20% of the total 1,000-ICBM force to which Nixon referred. A Minuteman III travels at more than 15,000 m.p.h. at an altitude of 700 miles. Flying over the Pole, it can reach its target in the Soviet Union in less than half an hour.

Ten Minuteman IIIs are under the immediate control of the "launch facility" called Tango Zero. Tango is situated on a farm 80 miles northwest of Great Falls. Aboveground the launch facility appears to be an elongated, plain, fenced-in house. Belowground lie two connected "capsules," rooms shaped like medicine capsules; one is the equipment room, the other, sealed behind an 8½-ton blast door, is the room where a two-man crew, sitting at two separate "status consoles," receives messages and stares at boards of lights. On June 6 this year, the command crew was 1st Lieut. Donald R. ("Skip") MacKinnon, 32, and 1st Lieut. Stephen J. Griffin, 24. June 6 was an atypically busy day for them because the launching codes were being changed, as they are periodically. A Diet Pepsi can rested on one of the consoles. Five miles away from Tango Zero, a Minuteman III "floats" in a vertical underground cylinder, pointed upward, held in place by mechanical "articulating arms" that look like four sets of three fingers. The missile is hospital green; no U.S. flag is painted on its side.

If a U.S. President were to begin launch procedures, he would signal the Strategic Air Command headquarters near Omaha, which would send messages with an "enabling code" to places like Tango Zero. The enabling code allows the missiles to be unlocked. MacKinnon and Griffin then open a red metal box containing a book that verifies the code received, along with two small keys. The six-figure code is dialed into a machine, and the missile's "safety" removed. Standing 12 ft. apart, the two crewmen then turn their keys within no more than 1.5 sec. of each other (it is impossible for a single person to turn both keys) and hold them in place for 5 sec. In another launch facility, another two-man crew performs the same procedure simultaneously. When all this is done, the missile lifts off.

The farm on which the procedure would take place belongs to Everett King, a burly man in his late 30s whose face is sun-red from his cap line down. King is less troubled by the capsules in his land than by a rabid skunk in the area that might threaten his children, and by a raccoon that commandeered the basketball backboard over the garage and will not back off. Besides missiles and Air Force personnel, King's 5,000 acres contain spring wheat and fallow land in alternating green and brown stripes, a crop of oats, malting barley, a sleepy horse, a donkey and a 60-mile view extending to the Rockies. On a late-spring afternoon, the mountains glow like dark ice.

King sees the presence of the missiles as an unfortunate necessity. "Anyway, nobody's safe from 'em anywhere." He does not spend his days worrying over nuclear war but he is almost certain one is coming. "You've got all those toys around. Someone's going to fool with them sooner or later. Look at Hiroshima. The Bomb was already used once. Things are building all the time. The Middle East, Central America. I listen to the radio a lot when I drive my tractor, and they were just sayin' the other day that there was—what was the name of that country? Pakistan—they were sayin' that Pakistan might get the Bomb. So nobody's safe. No, I don't mind the missiles on my land. If they go off, it'll probably happen at night. I'll never know."

The most likely circumstances under which nuclear war would occur, says Nixon, are the following: 1) an accident, 2) proliferation, 3) a small war in which U.S. and Soviet interests collide, 4) a miscalculation by one superpower of the other's interests, 5) a Soviet pre-emptive strike against China: "They cannot allow China to gain sufficient nuclear strength." Elaborating on the small-war theory, Nixon says it is unlikely that a nuclear conflict would be ignited in either Afghanistan ("too far away for us") or in Central America ("too far away for them"). The most probable place would be the Middle East. "But, you know, the Russians might be a little goosey about going in there because they could think, 'Those Israelis have a Masada complex.' Someone pushes the Israelis, the Israelis might just *bomb* the bastards!"

Nixon's office is much hotter now; the air conditioning is missed. Outside, an early Fourth of July celebrator has set off a brief volley of Chinese firecrackers. By nightfall the East River will be ablaze with rockets.

"I found a far different world and a far different presidency in 1969 than when I left the Eisenhower Administration in January 1961. In these respects: first, the overwhelming superiority that the U.S. had over the Soviet Union in terms of nuclear weapons was gone. In 1961 we had a first-strike capability. That was gone. The Soviet Union was not yet ahead of us, but they certainly were equal to us. In the campaign, I made the point that we must be No. 1. I made the point not out of an appeal to ego, but because I remembered what superiority had meant to us when we had it. I felt it was very important that the Soviets *not* have it. But in the interests of avoiding nuclear coercion, we had to have sufficiency, which meant parity. And what parity meant for nuclear diplomacy was this: the U.S. had to develop a nuclear strategy to deal with the world as if nuclear weapons did not *exist.*

"So in 1969 we saw a different world in terms of the nuclear power balance. We saw a different world in the relationship between China and the Soviet Union. The split between the two had really begun in 1959, but U.S. policies had not changed one bit. Now there was no question that a split had occurred. And then the U.S. was involved in the war in Viet Nam. So I had three priorities on becoming President: to change the relationship with China, to change the relationship with the Soviet Union and to bring the war in Viet Nam to an end. What I had in mind was a three-track approach to those problems. I wanted to end the Viet Nam War in a way that would be consistent with U.S. foreign policy interests. I was *not* seeking, as some unsophisticated or partisan critics have maintained, better relationships with China and the Soviet Union *because* of Viet Nam. I was seeking them as ends in themselves. It seemed to me very important for us to develop a new relationship with the Soviet Union because of the shift in the nuclear balance. And I was thinking not only of China then, but of China in the next century, and of the future balance of power among the U.S., China and the Soviets.

"To achieve those ends, I had also to consider how to end that war in Viet Nam. One of the options was the nuclear option, in other words, massive escalation: either bombing the dikes or the nuclear option. Of course, there was a third option: withdrawal. Get out. Blame Viet Nam on the Democrats. I rejected the withdrawal option because it would have been inconsistent with our foreign policy interests. At the other end of the spectrum, I ruled out bombing the dikes and the nuclear option. I rejected the bombing of the dikes, which would have drowned 1 million people, for the same reason that I rejected the nuclear option. Because the targets presented were not military targets. Nobody was exactly saying, 'Pave 'em over!' the way our friend in the Air Force, [General Curtis] LeMay, would have suggested. But I didn't see any targets in North Viet Nam that could not have been as well handled by conventional weapons.

"And then the other reason for my rejecting massive escalation: because I was convinced that it would destroy any chances for moving forward with the Soviets and China. So we went with a program of Vietnamization, which we coupled with withdrawal, which we coupled with military pressure, nonnuclear, which we coupled with the negotiating track. We went on all four tracks. And we wound up with not the most satisfactory solution in 1973, but it was a solution."

He frowns and shrugs. In rapid succession he looks perplexed, annoyed, engaged.

"There were three other instances when I considered using nuclear weapons. One was in the '73 war, when Brezhnev threatened to intervene unilaterally in the Mideast. We could not allow Israel to go down the tube. We could not allow the Soviets to have a predominant position in the region. That had to be the bottom line. I wanted to send that message, and putting the weapons on alert did that. We did not so much want to threaten the Soviet Union with nuclear weapons as to indicate that the U.S. would resist them, conventional and nuclear. That was my decision. There's been a lot of second-guessing that it was someone else's. It was mine.

"A second time involved China. There were border conflicts. Henry [Kissinger, then National Security Adviser in the Nixon Administration] used to come in and talk about the situation. Incidentally, this was before the tapes. You won't have these on the tapes." He continues without changing his expression. "Henry said, 'Can the U.S. allow the Soviet Union to jump the Chinese?'—that is, to take out their nuclear capability. We had to let the Soviets know we would not tolerate that.

"Finally, there was 1971, the Indo-Pak war. After Mrs. Gandhi completed the decimation of East Pakistan, she wanted to gobble up West Pakistan. At least that's the way I read it. The Chinese were climbing the walls. We were concerned that the Chinese might intervene to stop India. We didn't learn till later that they didn't have that kind of conventional capability. But if they did step in, and the Soviets reacted, what would *we* do? There was *no question* what we would have done."

He is in high gear now. He does not sound like a man out of office. He emphasizes that the entire history of nuclear diplomacy under the Eisenhower, Kennedy and Nixon administrations led to a narrowing of the nuclear option. Thus the only way out for the superpowers is arms control, but "arms control must not be sought as a goal in

itself. Far more important is our political understanding of
the Soviets." For Nixon, this is where things get interesting, where the country gets interesting. Odd to realize that
Nixon's America is not home and hearth, not the Fourth of
July. It is a European empire, removed from Europe and
without imperial designs, yet still the world's main player

Should nuclear weapons be abolished? Impossible, he
says. Without nuclear weapons the U.S. would always be a
superpower because of its economy. But the Soviet Union
would not be a superpower without the Bomb. In any case,
the point is moot.

A weapons freeze? He sees a freeze as a "naive approach to a very complex problem. A freeze at present levels would leave the Soviets in a position of superiority."

Should the U.S. concentrate its arsenal on defensive
weapons? He says that he favors the Strategic Defense Ini-
tiative (otherwise known as Star Wars), but that population defense would not be functional until the next century. "So what do we do about *this* century, in which we all
live and some of us will die?" He offers one more list:

"First, lengthen the nuclear fuse. Strengthen our conventional capability in Europe. Deter all the way up the
line.

"Second, the U.S. should alter its basic weapons strategy from targeting populations to a counterforce capability.
That goes against those who support the idea of mutual as-
sured destruction as a deterrent. But I think MAD is obso-
lete. What American President is going to risk New York
and Chicago to save Berlin? As I look back on World War
II and on the war in the Pacific, I think the whole concept

of targeting civilian populations was morally wrong. In World War I, there were 16 million deaths. In World War II, there were 55 million. Much of the difference was that targets were noncombatants. I strongly believe that we should move away from the concept of massive destruction of cities and toward military targets. It's a better deterrent, a better chance to create stability.

"You see, I'm not talking about *winning.* I'm talking about the world as it is. The rivalry between the U.S. and the Soviet Union can be managed but not eliminated. That's the kind of world we live in."

He plants his feet on the carpet between the ottoman and the chair, folds his arms on his knees and stares hard at his listener.

"The United States was meant to be a great power. De Gaulle said that France was never her true self unless she was engaged in a great enterprise. Since World War II, the U.S. *has* been engaged in a great enterprise. It has been good for us, internally, to feel that way. The moment we turn isolationist, it will be disastrous for the rest of the world. But in the long run, it will be disastrous for us too. We will become self-centered, introverted. As I look at young people these days, I see that each can make a difference in the world. Not just in his own family. Not just in his community. Not just in his country. But the whole *world.* I think Americans are very lucky to have the problems they have."

On July 4, 1985, would Richard Nixon say that the world is a safer place than on July 4, 1945?

"Yes."

Then, was Hiroshima, in some way, good for the world?

"Yes."

WHAT
THE PEOPLE SAW

The potential significance of Hiroshima was never lost on Americans. Even bathed in the kissing and weeping at the end of the war, people realized that the remarkable Bomb that felled an empire and brought the world to rapt attention was not going to be a gift without a price. In the Aug. 20, 1945, issue of *Time,* James Agee looked ahead: "With the controlled splitting of the atom, humanity, already profoundly perplexed and disunified, was brought inescapably into a new age in which all thoughts and things were split—and far from controlled." Agee was anticipating an opposition between people and their invention that would widen rapidly as the century continued, until eventually Americans would almost come to believe that the Bomb had invented itself. The new age would be seen not as a time of what people did, but of what was done to them. Forty years now we have been living in that age, no longer new, yet nothing has replaced it. Those born in the atomic age most likely will die in the atomic age, if they do not die because of it. What people saw in Hiroshima was not only the suffering of people; the devastation of a city; the conclusion of a long and deadly war; the development of a scientific-military partnership; a new set of rules for U.S. Presidents and for international politics. It was a vision of the future, a forecast of the world's destruction. We did not like what we saw.

We therefore went about the business of accommodating that unhappy vision, and avoiding it at the same time. Both ends were achieved in the culture, where the collective consciousness could make its fears decorative. Ever since Hiroshima, the Bomb has been at the center of films, books, plays, paintings, songs, intellectual life. It has not always played the same part. In the years immediately after Hiroshima, the public seemed not to want to confront the Bomb directly, and so created a culture in which the end of the world was given a sidelong glance. Lately, we cannot seem to get enough of the Bomb, and stare with a hypnotic fixation.

In a way, the world of politics brought about both extreme reactions because the Bomb, of necessity, was kept secret from the public before it was first used and, perhaps of necessity, has been treated by those in charge of it as a secret ever since. What are secrets to governments are mysteries to the public; no one outside of a very few people in power has ever understood how nuclear weapons are developed, or why. Suddenly there was Hiroshima, suddenly the hydrogen bomb, suddenly the MIRVs. Yet while the machinations of the experts and professionals have remained hidden from the public, the effects of the weapons have been continually described and displayed. In the space between secret processes and demonstrated effects, the public imagination has produced works in which the ends were always clear, and thus focused upon, and the means obscure, and thus ignored.

What people saw initially in Hiroshima seems to have scared them more profoundly than they realized they could be scared. In 1946, W.H. Auden coined the term the age of anxiety. But anxiety did not begin to plumb the peculiar fear engendered by the Bomb: not only the image of world death, unwarned of, unsignaled, but of death-in-life, benumbed survivors of an atomic explosion wandering poisoned and helpless as the Hiroshima citizens Yoshitaka Kawamoto saw the morning of the bombing. Or, less dramatically, wandering in a world so near the brink of atomic war that they could no longer live freely and wholeheartedly, a world in which it feels dead to be alive. Yale Professors Robert J. Lifton and Kai Erikson defined the psychological boundaries of that world: "The question so often asked, 'Would the survivors envy the dead?' may turn out to have a simple answer. No, they would be incapable of such feelings. They would not so much envy as, inwardly and outwardly, resemble the dead."

Responding to such an image, American culture of the late 1940s and early 1950s absorbed a whole range of fictional characters who were at once alive, dead and menacing. Frankenstein, created by Mary Shelley in 1818, came into his own. The Frankenstein movies starring Boris Karloff were produced in the 1930s, but not until 20 years later, when these films found a showcase on television, did the American imagination fully respond. Like the Dracula, mummy and zombie films of the same period, which were almost equally popular, the Frankenstein story was not only of the living dead, but contained the additional element of science run amuck, which allowed another connection to be made to nuclear threat. Here was the atomic tale writ wild. Brilliant Dr. Frankenstein, tampering with nature, gums up an experiment intended to safeguard life and make men immortal, and suddenly a little girl lies dead in the monster's arms. Not since Daedalus had a technological feat backfired more painfully.

King Kong was also revived as part of the folklore of the era, eliciting an audience's sympathies by representing a force taken out of nature and abused. The innocent atom wore a gorilla suit. But new figures arose as well. Stories about whole galaxies demolished by radiation were common; the Japanese, as if performing for Americans the dual function of accusation and exculpation, produced dozens of English-dubbed movies about radioactive monsters from the sky or the deep. More subtle were such films as *Invasion of the Body Snatchers*, which simultaneously confronted the fear of death-in-life and embraced it; people might be better off devoid of emotions (read normal life). The effect was to make a pre-emptive strike against the Bomb.

It is even possible to see the films of the early 1950s not

just as anti-Bomb, but anti-Communist. The nation was being told that it was better to be dead than Red, with the implication that the two conditions were indistinguishable. Thus images of de-spirited human beings may have represented victims of a dual menace. In practical terms the two threats could be viewed as one and the same; surrender to the Soviet way of life, which was seen as death-in-life, would first entail a nuclear war. The central danger of the undead creatures—that they had expansionist tendencies to make the entire world undead—may have cooperated nicely with the scares of the times.

Exceptions to these indirect dealings existed too. In 1958, Tom Lehrer was singing *We Will All Go Together When We Go* ("universal bereavement,/ an inspiring achievement"). Robert Lowell, ahead of his time in such things, wrote *Fall 1961:* "All autumn the chafe and jar/ of nuclear war;/ we have talked our extinction to death." Marguerite Duras's *Hiroshima, Mon Amour* might also be judged an exception to the indirectness of the period. In some respects, *Hiroshima, Mon Amour* is not about Hiroshima at all, only using the occasion as a locus for showing how people learn to deal with a tragic past—in the case of the woman in the story, a past that has nothing to do with Hiroshima. Yet choosing Hiroshima as the context, the witness box, for the woman's revelation is a way of saying: Here is the place one either remembers or forgets, and the consequence of forgetting is Hiroshima.

The majority reaction of the era, however, still was not to look squarely at what was feared. Literature took a very sidelong glance. In what other age would the perpetually haunted and displaced hero have emerged with such stature? In what other age would a writer like Kafka have been made so welcome: characters lost in and tormented by a gnostic society, unaware of the location and identities of their enemies, feeling peril and persecution for unspecified crimes, and yet not innocent either?

In the 1960s the indirect approach to the Bomb seemed to be changing. In 1963 Alfred Hitchcock's *The Birds* was produced, and in 1964 Stanley Kubrick's *Dr. Strangelove*. One was a standard something-is-wrong-with-nature film that made monsters of benignities, the other a headlong black-comic attack on the nuclear threat. Dr. Strangelove even incorporated the subtheme of nature out of control in the Bomb-crazy Dr. Strangelove's right arm, which goes its own way, fondly recalls the doctor's Nazi days and at one point attempts to strangle its "master." Commercially, if not critically, *The Birds* was the more successful of the two films, even though the character of the mad nuclear scientist (always suspect) became a permanent part of national folklore. Still, it seemed that we were not quite ready for so relentless a contemplation of nuclear disaster, especially one that began with the on-screen demurrer, "It is the stated position of the U.S. Air Force that their safeguards would prevent the occurrence of such events as are depicted in this film."

For the following decade, to the mid-1970s, the American public seemed to be supplied with diversions from the choice of either a direct or an indirect apprehension of the Bomb. One was the introduction into the culture of explicit sex and explicit violence—the explicitness seeming more significant than either sex or violence per se, and perhaps indicating a desire to take revenge on some threatening situation, if not the one that might have been uppermost in people's minds. Fictional heroes of the period may have offered similar distractions, functioning as little "bombs" in their own right. McMurphy of Ken Kesey's novel *One Flew Over the Cuckoo's Nest* and Yossarian of Joseph Heller's *Catch-22* were at war with the world, and both nuked the societies that sought to contain them. One took on the scientists, the other the military: a one-two punch for the common man. Perhaps these explosions were not diversions after all but more sophisticated signs of frustration with a world where one's possibilities seemed to be denied and threatened with extermination.

Then, too, perhaps we were no longer so troubled by the Bomb, the initial shock having worn off. Like Lowell, Americans may have grown weary of talking, or dreaming, their extinction to death. The '50s and early '60s, the time of the horror film, were also the time of bomb shelters and "duck and cover" instructions to schoolchildren, who, like Kawamoto in the '40s, were taught to hide under desks in a bombing attack. The combination of fright and absurdity might have been enough to put the Bomb on the shelf for a while.

And there was Viet Nam, destructive and tragic in all other respects, but in terms of the tensions of the atomic age, a possible source of relief. Americans were engaged in a conventional war again, difficult enough without thoughts of the Bomb.

But then, in the late 1970s, really for the first time in

more than 30 years, people started looking at the Bomb head on:

In art, Erika Rothenberg created an acrylic in 1982 called *Pushing the Right Buttons,* a painting of two buttons, the one on top labeled "Launch" and the one beneath it "Lunch." Alex Grey, in 1980, painted *Nuclear Crucifixion,* an oil on linen reminiscent of Matthias Grünewald's painting in the 16th century, except here Jesus is crucified in a mushroom cloud. Michael Smith and Alan Herman produced a mixed-media work in 1983 called *Government Approved Home Fallout Shelter Snack Bar,* a survivalist food counter for the prudent nuclear family, equipped with provisions and three stools. In 1981 Robert Morris created a huge work for the Hirshhorn Museum in Washington, titled *Jornado del Muerto,* after the site of the Trinity test. Morris' effort includes a drawing called *The Miyuki Bridge,* the bridge to which Kawamoto fled on Aug. 6, 1945, and photographs of Einstein and Oppenheimer juxtaposed with that of a torn and burned boy.

In the theater, Arthur Kopit wrote the *End of the World* in 1984, a serious comedy in which one of the characters says, "So I sometimes think, now it's all over and we're up there in the big debriefing space in the sky, and the good Lord decides to hold a symposium 'cause he's curious: How did this thing happen? And everybody says, 'Hey, don't look at me, I didn't wanna do it!' The end result being that everyone realizes *no* one wanted to do it!' " Other signs of the times are noisier. Video games enable players to nuke planets and stars. A rock group calls itself the B-52s. Who does not know the Grateful Dead? The literature produced about the Bomb in the past few years has created a small industry. There have been recent novels about the "end," notably Denis Johnson's *Fiskadoro*, a story of survival in a contaminated world, like Nevil Shute's 1957 best seller *On the Beach*. A book of drawings by atom-bomb survivors, *The Unforgettable Fire*, had great public impact in 1982 when the first American edition appeared. At least one major poet recently turned his hand to this subject. Robert Penn Warren's *New Dawn* chronicles the *Enola Gay's* mission from the takeoff on Tinian, to the flight over the Aioi Bridge—"Color/ Of the world changes. It/ Changes like a dream." The poem ends with an account of the flyers' celebrations, and then after:

Some men, no doubt, will, before sleep, consider
One thought: I am alone. But some,
In the mercy of God, or booze, do not

Long stare at the dark ceiling.
There is seemingly no end to the nonfiction works on this subject. Jonathan Schell's *The Fate of the Earth* seized broad public attention in 1982 and opened the way to hundreds of books a year since then on arms control, arms negotiations, plans for peace, manuals on how to survive nuclear catastrophes. In the past two or three years, an entire intellectual community has been born around the Bomb, a portable Algonquin Round Table (minus the wit) made up of such people as McGeorge Bundy, George Kennan, Harold Brown, Robert McNamara and several retired military leaders, many of whom were among the policymakers who

originally protected the secrecy of the Bomb and who have now gone public with strategic theories and proposals for arms limitations.

As these books and essays were being written, there were other diverse signs that the country was ready to look directly at the Bomb. Surveys begun in 1978 by John Mack, a psychiatrist at the Harvard Medical School, found that large percentages of schoolchildren experience a high degree of fear about impending nuclear war. Harvard's Robert Coles, the author of *Children of Crisis,* disputes such findings with research of his own. In Coles' studies the only children who worried inordinately about the Bomb were those whose parents were directly involved with antinuclear movements.

In 1983 the American Catholic bishops also addressed the nuclear issue squarely with their provocative pastoral letter: "The Challenge of Peace: God's Promise and Our Response." Erupting from a church history that either ignored nuclear weapons or, in the nationalistic enthusiasms of some clergymen, saw such weapons as new arms for Christian soldiers, the bishops suddenly leaped forward: "We cannot avoid our responsibility to lift up the moral dimensions of the choices before our world and nation." They emphasized that they were speaking purely from a moral pulpit, "as pastors, not politicians." No sooner had they spoken, however, than many conservative American Catholics, among others, faulted their logic: the moral issue of the Bomb could not be dissociated from political processes; the bishops were at best naive, at worst disingenuous. One direct assault evidently deserved another.

Television has offered the most direct and dramatic presentations of the Bomb in recent years. In 1983 the TV movie *The Day After* shook much of the public, at least for a short while, with scenes of missiles shooting out of silos in Kansas cornfields and of dazed Midwesterners bravely trying to go on in the aftermath of a nuclear assault. (Kawamoto's criticism of *The Day After* was that the survivors would never have been that alert.) Other new films and television movies like *Threads* have graphically shown devastated cities and families, bodies crushed by buildings, the disintegration of flesh. None of these works deals realistically (if at all) with the political processes by which a nuclear war might be started, only with the dire consequences. That is typical of most recent cultural representations. If the popular imagination refused to touch the Bomb 30 years ago, it seems desperate to embrace the thing today.

Of course, both types of reactions, being extremes, may have little to do with the real fears of people; that is, the private feelings of an individual that his life is in a constant state of jeopardy, and that there is no course available but to live either sybaritically or timorously until the occasion of the inevitable *boom.* Cultural manifestations of public feelings are not very hard to read, but people are a lot more complicated than the things they produce to rep resent them.

No film, book, play or game ever tells how seriously we take even our own ideas. It is possible that many of these works merely indicate how the public believes it ought to feel about the Bomb, or are part of the eschatological tendencies of any age.

Also, what appears to be antinuclear anger or trepidation in the country may simply be part of the perpetual up-and-down attitude toward technology in general. Drs. Frankenstein and Strangelove are monsters to the Luddite sensibility quite apart from thoughts of a nuclear winter. It may be that after Hiroshima, Americans were no longer so keen on their seemingly infinite capacity to make things work, that the technological success of Hiroshima took the heart out of American can-do self-esteem. (At Los Alamos, a code name for the Bomb was the "gadget.") On this basis, one might work up an elaborate psychological theory explaining the subsequent fall of America's industry and the rise of Japan's as products of a national guilty conscience. But the American impulse to deplore and fret over mechanical progress has always been as strong as the impulse to pursue it; we condemned the car, which we love, long before we condemned the Bomb.

As for the feeling of powerlessness the Bomb engenders, that may be no different from the feeling of powerlessness brought by the domination of the state. Since the state controls the Bomb, it is easy to link the two as the same source of discomfort, and since the power of the state and the Bomb grew up together, they may be confused unconsciously. The trouble is that so many threats are attached to modern life that even something as blatant as a nuclear weapon cannot always be distinguished in an array that includes every terror from cancer and insanity to a telephone call in the middle of the night.

Yet there can be no question that the Bomb's presence has abetted, if not exclusively accounted for, much of what is nerve-racking and unsatisfactory in the world: a feeling of dislocation; aimlessness; loneliness; dim perceptions of unidentified dangers. Once the Bomb was used and the enormity of its effects realized, it had the impact of Copernicus, Darwin, Freud—of any monumental historical theory that proved, fundamentally, how small people are, how accidental their prominence, how subject to external manipulation. When the Bomb dropped, people not only saw a weapon that could boil the planet and create a death-in-life; they saw yet one more proof of their impotence. We live in a world of "virile weapons and impotent men," wrote the French historian Raymond Aron shortly before his death in 1983. We saw a vision of the future in Hiroshima, but we also saw ourselves, and (again) we did not like what we saw.

So what is there to do about the Bomb, which may be reduced in numbers but not removed? The answer seems to be: nothing. Citizens of nations were introduced to the art of modern warfare by the institution of strategic bombing, but unfortunately they were introduced solely as targets. The only maneuverability given ordinary people is how they may think about the Bomb. Is it possible to do that less fearfully and more clearly? Americans do not really believe in the Apocalypse, no matter how many movies we watch. One way or another in the next few years, we will want to stop looking too indirectly or too directly, and quietly come to terms with the Bomb.

Coming to terms with the Bomb means first accepting a basic fact about nature. When the Bomb was dropped, much was made of how man had conquered nature, exposed its deepest mysteries; in a sense, how nature, like Japan, had been brought to its knees. Yet it did not take long for the realization to sink in that the splitting of the atom not only gave people no greater authority over nature than they had before, it proved how helpless they were when handling natural forces. Since that time, there seems to have been a general divorce of human life from other natural phenomena. It is as if people concluded that with atomic chain reactions nature played a trick on the world, and is no longer to be trusted as an ally.

Coming to terms with nature simply means coming to terms with its neutrality, and that ultimately means coming to terms with oneself. If some "trick" was played by nuclear fission, it was people who played the trick on themselves. In a lecture to fellow scientists, Oppenheimer said, "In some sort of crude sense which no vulgarity, no humor, no overstatement can quite extinguish, the physicists have known sin; and this is a knowledge which they cannot lose." Oppenheimer's presumption is that the physicists, as people, had not known sin before making the Bomb, which sounds like wishful confessing. Nature is what people choose to make of it.

This much we already know of ourselves: we kill one another, and from age to age we will always find instruments to suit that predisposition. In a way, the Bomb may have curbed the killer instinct because of the immensity of its power. People will not, cannot use absolutely any weapons they choose anymore. But the instinct is there still, storming back and forth like a shark beyond the reef. Whatever fears the Bomb has brought, the fear of our murderous capacities is deeper. However monstrous our visions of the Bomb's future, they were only mirrors of what we did, and would probably do again, if we could get away alive. Captain Robert Lewis, co-pilot of the *Enola Gay*, looked down on Hiroshima and asked, "My God, what have we done?" We did what we always do.

Yet coming to terms with oneself also means coming to terms with responsibilities. Taking responsibility for one's actions and decisions seems out of fashion in the atomic age, but in that *Time* article of Aug. 20, 1945, James Agee immediately saw that individual responsibility was at the heart of Hiroshima: "When the Bomb split open the universe and revealed the prospect of the infinitely extraordinary, it also revealed . . . that each man is eternally and above all else responsible for his own soul." Responsibility for one's own soul inevitably involves others, since no one judges the quality of his soul in isolation. If what we saw in Hiroshima was ourselves, we saw everyone else at the same time. Everybody lives in Hiroshima.

In the end we face a hard, self-evident fact: whether because we dropped the Bomb, or because we live in its shadow, or because we are able to use it, we have created an enormous handicap for ourselves, and we will have to learn to survive and endure in spite of that handicap. The handicap will not disappear. It only remains to be seen if we will disappear, or if, by an effort of will and judgment we can make our handicap work in our favor, never pretending that we are anything but imperfect, yet also understanding that imperfection is a state of grace, a gift tied directly to a perception of common humanity.

Suzuko Numata understands this effort. She is a tiny woman of 61 who, like Yoshitaka Kawamoto, was not far from the hypocenter when the atom bomb exploded. Like Kawamoto, Numata devotes much of her time to speaking to schoolchildren about her experiences on Aug. 6. She spends her private hours in her orderly, sun-filled house on a canal, tending a small garden bright with hydrangeas, peonies, red camelias, sweet daphne and amaryllis; and taking care of several cats and a large, cheerful doll that sits near the porch and whose outfits she changes according to the seasons. Numata smiles easily when she talks. She enjoys watching the ballet on television, and she moves her hands to the steps of the dancers.

She grew up in Hiroshima, the eldest daughter in a family of five. She took lessons on the harp and in folk dance and ballet. "I loved to dance. My dancing made my parents happy." Like all Japanese young women at that time, Numata anticipated a life of marriage and children, and she was engaged to marry a soldier. The wedding was planned for some time shortly after Aug. 8, 1945, when her fiancé was expected home on leave.

When the Bomb fell, Numata, then 21, was working in a military communications office. The building collapsed in the explosion, and her left ankle was severed. That night she was taken to a hospital, where she remained for three days with no doctor, no nurse or medicine. Her left leg became gangrenous. She believed she was going to die. She hoped that her fiancé would visit her, but, as she learned from his parents a few days later, the young man had been killed in action in July. Her third day in the hospital, a doctor came, examined her leg and told her that it would have to be amputated to save her life.

"I said, 'Doctor, if I lose my leg, I will never be married, never work again.' And the doctor said, 'You are not the only patient here. Think hard about your choice by the time I return.' I was in despair. All I ever hoped for was to be taken away in a single act. I *wanted* to die."

In the dark, Numata heard the voices of three other victims, who advised her what to do. The first voice spoke gibberish; "I could not even make out if it was the voice of a man or woman." The second voice was somewhat clearer but faint. She could not understand what that voice was saying either.

"The third person, too, was gasping. But I could hear the words. He said, 'All of us here are going to die at any moment. But *you* ... if your leg is amputated, you still would live. *Live.* Take the operation, and *live.*'

"So I decided, and I said, 'Bring the doctor.' "